THE COVENTRY WE HAVE LOST

FORGOTTEN FOLESHILL

(Including Longford, Bell Green, Hawkesbury, Alderman's Green & Stoney Stanton Road)

Manufacture de J. & J. CASH, LTD., à COVENTRY.

Cash's Factory, Cash's Lane, Foleshill, 1910 (Waterman)
(Featured on a New Year's postcard from Cash's Paris office)

David Fry & Albert Smith

Simanda Press
Berkswell 2018

These three items have been taken from various editions of the Coventry Graphic. The first dates from 6 February 1914, the second from 22 August 1913 and the third from 23 March 1912.

Dangerous Canal Bridges.

Graphic photos.

BRIDGE ON THE ALDERMAN'S GREEN ROAD TO BULKINGTON. About 11ft. wide.

BRIDGE ON THE FOLESHILL ROAD LEADING TO THE DAIMLER WORKS.

DOUBLE BRIDGES AT BLACK-HORSE LANE. 12ft. wide and very steep.

Photo by E. W. Appleby.

Daudi Chwa Kabaka, the young King of Buganda, and three members of his suite, who paid a visit to the Standard Motor Works, Foleshill Road, on Friday last. They made a complete inspection of the works and expressed delight with their visit. The King has ordered a Standard car. On the left of the picture are Mr. R. W. Maudslay, managing director of the Standard Co., and Mr. Sturrock, the King's tutor, and on the extreme right is Mr. J. Budge, manager to the company.

FOR SALE.—Two important-looking Freehold Villas, Nos. 130 and 132, Foleshill Road ; short distance from Daimler ; on tram route ; 1d. stage to town ; good position for doctor or professional gentleman. Two thirds of capital left on at 4 per cent. reduces the best villa to £20 yearly rent.—Apply Rockland Works, Eagle Street.

Contents

The Coventry We Have Lost: Forgotten Foleshill

Foleshill is the largest and the most complex of Coventry's suburbs. It has not had a clear centre for some time if indeed it ever did. The scatter of hamlets across the parish that has characterised its geography since medieval times have now becomes centres for various modern suburbs in themselves. Foleshill was also the most independent of Coventry's surrounding parishes as it lacked a dominant landowner to limit its development. This explains why, more than other suburbs, its industrial past and present have intermingled with its housing.

The area known as Foleshill has existed since at least Saxon times when its land formed part of the estates of Lady Godiva. It is possible that its name, 'the hill of the people' was connected to a landscape feature near the medieval church of St Lawrence in Old Church Road. Today, however, most Coventrians associate Foleshill with the line of Foleshill Road to the west of the parish. Foleshill's original southern boundary was just north of Cash's Lane, but as many people today assume it starts at the bottom of Foleshill Road, by the ring road, this book includes that area as well. The whole length of Stoney Stanton Road has also been included, although like the Foleshill Road it has almost taken on the character of an area in itself, but for much of its length has always been part of Foleshill parish. The road's southern ex-parochial stretch is mainly part of a larger area known as Harnall. Overall this large parish covers about five miles by three miles at its widest points.

The previous book in this series on Coventry's suburbs dealt with Earlsdon and Chapelfields and the contrast with Foleshill could not be greater. In terms of size, those suburbs covered an area barely two miles by one mile. Both Earlsdon and Chapelfields were artificial creations of the mid-nineteenth century; each planned and developed over a relatively short period of time as nucleated settlements. Foleshill is a much greater area that has been shaped by developments over more than a thousand years. Settlements were spread out along its various roads and lanes working against the evolution of any single focus. Only in the twentieth century with the development of the tram routes and the spread of housing has it become a more homogeneous suburb, but still too large in itself to be a coherent whole.

It is easy to see Foleshill's later nineteenth and twentieth development as being disorganised and piecemeal and it is true that there was no general overall plan. By looking a little deeper the miscellaneous streets can often be seen to be part of larger estates, created by a particular developer with specific architectural characteristics and identity. Many of the historic hamlets have retained their own separate sense of identity within greater Foleshill. This book has tried to emphasise some of those characteristics; an important feature of all *The Coventry We Have Lost* Books. The photographs, large-scale maps and newspaper clippings used are deliberately chosen from the early twentieth century. This was a time of transition where countryside, cottages and centuries old rural ways rubbed shoulders with the new routines of life in newly built factories and housing estates. It was also a time when there was a greater community involvement outside the home, often centred on the local church or chapel. With the introduction of more holidays and longer weekends people had time for enjoying sports and hobbies and this is reflected in the many surviving group photographs that record these activities. It is impossible in a book as short as this to do full justice to the story of Foleshill given its size and complex history. Each of its sections could easily be developed into a book of its own, but hopefully, it does give a taste of the fascinating story of what is one of the most interesting and diverse of Coventry's suburbs.

FREEHOLD LAND,
FOLESHILL.

TO BE SOLD BY AUCTION,

Together, or in such Lots as may be determined upon, on the 15th day of March next, (unless previously disposed of by Private Contract,) at the NEW INN, Foleshill, between the Hours of Four and Five o'Clock in the Afternoon,

A MOST valuable Piece of GROUND, containing about 2 Acres, more or less, situate on the right hand side of the Turnpike road leading from Coventry to Bedworth, between the Wheat Sheaf Public House and New Inn Bridge. This Property is most advantageously circumstanced for building, and the lower end of it, adjoining the Coventry Canal, might be converted into a Wharf with very great advantage.

Mr. DANIEL STONEY, of Foleshill, will show the Land; and to treat for the purchase, and for further particulars, apply to Mr. E. D. DICKENS, Solicitor, Coventry, who has several sums of MONEY to advance, on approved security.

Coventry, 19th February, 1824.

Coventry Herald, 20 February 1824

It is clear from this advertisement of the important role the canal played in the development of Foleshill. Selling off parcels of land that adjoined both the canal and the main roads was not only a profitable business for the landowner but attracted economic activity to the area

James Bearsley is a weaver. Prisoner came to him on the morning of the 30th of August last, and asked him to buy a watch, which he had found the preceding day on the Foleshill road, and which he had been unable to find a owner for. Witness looked at it, and perceiving the arms of the Odd Fellows, said he had no doubt he could find the owner. Prisoner said he had rather sell it, out and out. Witness told him if he would wait a few minutes, he would take it to the house where the Lodge was held. He accordingly went to Smith's, who owned the watch, and sent for a constable, who took prisoner into custody.

Ann Bateman, the widow of the constable, produced the watch, which she had had in her possession ever since her husband's death. Mr. Smith identified it.

The Jury returned a verdict of *Guilty*, and sentence of death was recorded against the prisoner.

Coventry Herald, 31 March 1826

It is not easy to get into the mind of the nineteenth century resident of Foleshill. The idea that life was cheap cannot but be reinforced by the knowledge of incidents like that in this news report.

Acknowledgements

Most of the photographs are from the authors' own collections, however, the following people and organisations kindly allowed some of their own illustrations to be used; Les Neil, the late Iris Collier and the late Celia Grew who have always been generous in allowing access to their postcard collections. May Jenkins page 51, Edgwick Poultry Farm; David Aston page 94, house in Stoney Stanton Road; Coventry History Centre (extracts from the Coventry Graphic); Warwick Record Office page 51, Foleshill Road. For anyone who wants to do their own research we are very lucky to have the well-resourced Coventry History Centre at the Herbert. Without those resources and the support of the knowledgeable staff this book could not have been written. (For further information on sources for carrying out your own research see page 99). Also, the authors are grateful for the help of Jayne and Anselm Gurney as well as John Payne for commenting on the text. All responsibility for any errors is ours; do please point them out. Contact dave@thecoventrywehavelost.co.uk with any comments or queries. Book layout was by Ian Wells, and the book was printed by Buy My Print info@buymyprint.co.uk

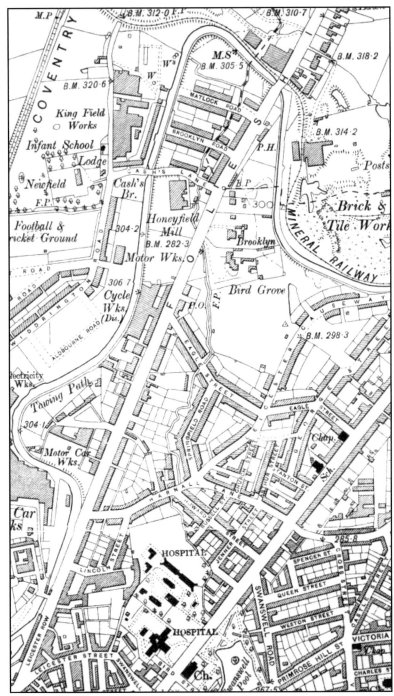

1906 Ordnance Survey Six Inch Map

At the start of Foleshill Road, by the canal basin, is a sign 'Welcome to Foleshill' and for many Coventrians that is what they think of as the start of the suburb. In fact this section of Foleshill Road lies almost entirely outside the historic Foleshill parish but, as explained in the introduction, it represents what many people today think of as Foleshill. The importance of the route was recognised when it was turnpiked in the middle of the eighteenth century by the Coventry to Hinckley Turnpike Trust. This created the very straight road we know today, before it was just a track over the heathland and wastes before reaching Longford. As with all turnpikes a fee was charged for all traffic to cover the cost of the improvements and so a toll gate was installed at the top of Bishop Street. A little more than ten years later saw the Coventry Canal being built with the canal basin now alongside the toll gate. The first stretch of the canal up to the Prince William Henry Bridge followed the line of the road on its west side. Until the 1890s there were very few houses by lower Foleshill Road.

Towards the end of the nineteenth century Coventry's economy began to boom and Foleshill offered the most easily accessible route for expansion. As a result we find factories and housing alongside one another to a greater extent than is found elsewhere in the city. In other areas that were developed later a greater attempt was made to create separate residential and industrial zones. By the First World War both sides of Foleshill Road had been flanked by terraced housing to just beyond Eagle Street. The looping canal to the west offered a rather awkward area of land for development behind the houses, but it was gradually occupied by various factories and some, like the O'Brien cycle works, also fronted the road.

Both Harnall Lane and Cash's Lane are part of the old pre-industrial network of roads in this area. All other roads are the product of developments from 1890 to 1910, such as Lincoln Street, Eagle Street, Brooklyn Road and Matlock Road. Apart from Lincoln Street most streets to the east of lower Foleshill Road were rarely developed as single streets. They were part of a series of small housing estates that exploited the original fields between the canal to the north and Harnall Lane to the east.

The agricultural history of the area lives on in the boundaries of some these estates as development land was frequently parcelled up for sale using the original field boundaries, accounting for some of the eccentric shapes. The story of a small sample of these estates will be explored in this section.

The importance of the Coventry Canal to the whole Foleshill area cannot be underestimated. Its excavation was completed in a relatively short time, starting in May 1768 near Longford and simultaneously working north and south of that point. Construction as far as Coventry to Bedworth was completed by August 1769. The canal brought an extra dimension to the economy of Foleshill by providing work at the wharfs that developed near many of the road crossings. More importantly, it aided the transport of coal for those collieries in the Hawkesbury area and beyond, helping them to flourish and provide one of the main sources of employment in the parish. As well as providing a new form of communication it also disrupted the old routes by cutting off some long-established routes. This can still be seen today at Lady Lane in Longford and Spring Road in Little Heath. It continued to be an influence in the twentieth century as many factories chose to locate alongside the canal for its value in bulk transportation. Its importance was diminished by the growth of road and rail traffic and there were plans to fill it in after the Second World War.

Electricity Goods Wharf, Coventry Canal, Coventry
Graphic
4 July 1913

The two clippings shown here are taken from Coventry's first weekly illustrated news magazine. They show that the Coventry Canals continued to play an important role in the Foleshill economy despite the existence of nearby railway lines. The Power Station in Sandy Lane was built beside the canal in 1894 as an efficient way of receiving bulk supplies of coal from the nearby Exhall Colliery. The power station discharges created so much heat from its operations that the canal water was always warm and therefore popular with local swimmers.

One of the most interesting sights to be seen during a walk along the canal bank is the unloading of the canal barges at the Electricity Works wharf. The expeditious method with which the fuel is thrown in the endless chain, and carried up into the building is a wonderful example of modern mechanical regularity and consistency. The illustration shows the machines at work. From the chain seen, or more properly gatherer the coal is dropped into a cross conveyer, and then into the elevators, and finally into the bunkers. The small gatherer on the left is a separate arrangement, and fills another set of bunkers.

Midland Water Ways.

UNLOADING BARGES AT THE COVENTRY CANAL WHARF, FOLESHILL ROAD.

THE CANAL NEAR PRINCE WILLIAM HENRY BRIDGE.

The view on the left shows activity by the canal basin while that on the right is the back of the recently expanded Courtaulds factory. It demonstrates the continuing importance of the canals at the beginning of the twentieth century to Coventry newest industries. The canal was widened at this point to deal with the congestion that the traffic created in delivering coal and chemicals to the new factory. Courtaulds even had their own canal boats to dump their chemical waste near Hawkesbury.

Foleshill Road, looking south towards Leicester Row 1949 (Richard Bailey)

Snow scene, looking south near Lincoln Street c1935 (Bill Sutton)

Looking north from Harnall Lane c1910 (F T Steele)

These three views give a feel for what the start of Foleshill Road looked like. The first two show the same section of Foleshill Road looking south, the other is facing north. The west side of the road was impossible to build on with the canal just over the fence, hidden by the advertising hoardings. The hoardings appear not to have survived the war in good order. The first houses on that side were built beyond Harnall Lane shown in the view at the bottom, with posters across their side wall. Harnall Lane itself is just to the right. None of the buildings in the foreground or the middle distance exists today having been replaced by various commercial redevelopments. The snow scene shows Lincoln Street to the middle left with housing on the left side all the way to the canal basin. Until the last decade of the nineteenth century, there would have been no houses at all on this stretch of Foleshill Road, as the city ended abruptly at the Draper's Field canal basin. The success of the various engineering industries in Coventry from the 1880s meant the city enjoyed a rapid growth so that by the 1890s building began to spill over into the countryside. With restrictions on development around the city's southern boundary, expansion along Foleshill Road offered an easy outlet.

War damage as shown in the top view and subsequent redevelopment has left this area unrecognisable today. The road has widened and the area had been dominated by retail and manufacturing units, but new housing alongside the canal has brought residential life back to lower Foleshill.

Lincoln Street 1907 (E.R.)

This was one of the first suburban side streets developed off lower Foleshill Road. It was also one of Edwin Stidworthy's first projects having applied for building consent for 17 houses in 1898. Over the next three decades he was responsible for many other developments across Coventry during this boom time in Coventry's growth. The street forms a dog-leg between Foleshill Road and Harnall Lane made up of two rows of terraced housing; the one shown here leads down to Harnall Lane in the distance. The masonry name-plate 'Southpool Terrace' can be seen on the top left of the first house, an attempt to give status to these inexpensive houses that do not have the benefit of front gardens that their neighbours on Foleshill Road had. Even worse for the inhabitants was to look out on the large Challenge (later Premier) Cycle Works, on the opposite side of the road.

Thornhill Road c1912 (Anon.)

An example of a slightly later but more salubrious residential development was that of Ena, Newland and Thornhill Roads, off Leicester Causeway. This 'U' shaped estate was planned by Coventry solicitor Charles Band in 1906. Typically for the period, having bought the land, he then got permission to lay out the roads and install basic services but did not build the houses. The land was then sold off in plots to various building firms to make his profit. The builders would be required to construct the houses on the same building line and a similar terraced style, but with individual variations allowed. This process can be seen in the postcard above, produced within a few years of the completion of the street. Some have bay windows and other not. However, by comparison with Lincoln Street, all houses have a front garden and those on the right, who did not get a bay window, have a sapling in the front garden instead.

Band Sergeant William Arthur Wareham's Military Funeral, Foleshill Road, Monday 22 June 1914 (F C Hancox)

Coventry was occasionally the scene of military funerals as a consequence of having the 7th (Territorial) Battalion of the Royal Warwickshire Regiment Barracks based in the city. Band Sergeant William Wareham was only 37 when he died from pleurisy. He had been a member of the regiment since he joined at the age of ten as a drummer boy. He was noted later for his solo performances on a cornet. This was a family affair as his father was the Regimental Colour Sergeant. They were both part-time (territorial) soldiers, which was an attractive proposition with the extra status and income it provided. In civilian life both father and son worked as coal merchants in Foleshill.

Accompanying the cortege was a hundred members of the battalion, together with the regimental band and a firing party of 13 with arms reversed. They paraded from William's home at 33 Foleshill Road to the London Road Cemetery, via the centre of town. The top view shows the coffin being placed on the gun carriage outside the Wareham's house, which was near the junction with Harnall Lane. The chimneys of Sandy Lane power station can be seen beyond the advertising hoardings alongside the canal. The middle view captures the cortege passing the entrance to Lincoln Street with the rest of the military procession stretching back up Foleshill Road with a tram at the rear. Band Sergeant Wareham had two children Arthur, aged nine and Olive, seven. However, his wife, Amy was seriously ill at the time of his death and was unable to attend the ceremony. The bottom view, also by the Lincoln Street junction, shows the members of the firing party flanking the band.

These photographs were taken by another long-serving member of the regiment, Fred Hancox, who was also a prolific amateur photographer. We are fortunate that his original plates still survive showing many aspects of Coventry's Edwardian life.

Foleshill Road 1906 (E.R.)

The large tree on the left of this view can be seen in the middle distance of the bottom photograph on page 9 with the barely discernible chimney at Courtaulds in the distance. The view shows the stretch of road leading up to the junction with Eagle Street on the distant right. None of these houses exist today, most having been destroyed in the war and those odd ones that remained have been demolished. A few larger houses were built in the first flush of development of this area but were later swamped by the sea of terraced housing. One of these was Hazlewood, 143 Foleshill Road, behind the wall on the immediate left. At this time it was the home of James Hazlewood a local cycle manufacturer. By June 1914 it was leased to the Coventry district of the Amalgamated Society of Engineers who converted it into their offices and social club and remained as its base until the buildings were cleared in the 1960s.

A Group of Coventry's Oldest ASE Members, 143 Foleshill Road August 1919 (Anon.)

The ASE (Amalgamated Society of Engineers) was founded in 1851 and was one of the country's foremost engineering unions. Given the character of Coventry's industry for the previous half century, the union's presence in the city was guaranteed. To judge from the statistics given in the caption, thirty members sharing 1,369 years suggest they averaged more than 45 years membership each. The cause of the occasion is not clear but the fact that the union was to join similar ones in the following year to become the Amalgamated Engineering Union, was already being discussed. This seems a good enough reason to celebrate those who devoted a lifetime of commitment to the ASE. The photograph is likely to have been taken in the garden of Hazlewood the house referred to in the caption above.

Harnall Lane West 1907 (E.R.)

Harnall Lane was one of Foleshill's oldest roads, dating from at least the middle ages. By 1907 residential development of the lane from Foleshill Road to Swan Lane was almost complete. The view above is taken from near the Foleshill Road end, just past the Lincoln Street junction to the right. Today all the buildings on the left have gone, down to Five Ways in the distance, shown in more detail below.

Five Ways, Harnall Lane West 1907 (E.R.)

This remarkable photograph of Five Ways captures the history of this area in a way that the written word cannot do. It is made all the more poignant by the buildings no longer standing. Today this junction of five roads still exists; Leicester Causeway to the immediate left of the pub, Springfield Road further round to the left and then, stretching the geography, Springfield Place back a few paces with Howard Street on the opposite side of the Road - hence the five ways. The pub, in common with some neighbouring buildings, has the characteristic top-shop that betrays its origins as a silk weaver's cottage. Its transformation into a pub took place in the 1840s soon after it was built. This group of mid-nineteenth century housing shows in its variety the piecemeal development of the street. The interspersed weavers' top shops were part of that development when that industry was still flourishing in the city. The houses had survived well into the twentieth century but the pub was closed in 1981 and later demolished so joining the other houses in this view that had been demolished earlier. A Sikh temple now covers most of this site.

Springfield Brook

The River Sowe and a number of streams run through the Foleshill area, sometimes influencing territorial boundaries and development, either through the line of roads and pathways or, more latterly, in the shape of housing estates. The map indicates the path of one of the streams known as the Springfield Brook that passes through lower Foleshill to the edge of the city centre where it feeds into Swanswell Pool. It has travelled from its source in Keresley under various roads as well as the canal and the Coventry to Nuneaton railway. Its impact on housing development varied, but all had to take account of its presence in their planning. This can be seen most obviously in the shape of Springfield Road which had to take a dog leg course to respect the brook. This is also seen in the Lant estate off Stoney Stanton Road, developed in the 1850s. Restrictions in its southern boundary challenged the developers to make the most efficient use of the awkward shape (see page 86). Springfield Brook also defined a more important boundary, that of Foleshill parish itself. From where it crossed Narrow Lane (Kingfield Road) through to Cash's Lane the stream separated Foleshill from the ancient Holy Trinity parish including the district of Radford.

Springfield Road 1907 (E.R.)

In the 1890s, after thirty years of economic stagnation, Coventry's industry was beginning to pick up speed and the space for housing was most easily available in the lower Foleshill area. Springfield Road was being laid out from 1893, from Harnall Lane to Eagle Street. The road dog-legged to the right, behind the children, echoing the path of the Springfield Brook running along the bottom of the gardens of the houses to the left. Those houses, as in Lincoln Street, did not have front gardens whereas those on the right are built to a slightly higher specification. The variety of houses in a terraced street is often subtle but is nearly always present as few streets were created entirely by just one builder. The photographer is standing in Harnall Lane, at the Five Ways junction where his presence has encouraged a group of schoolchildren to gather in the road (always good for later sales of the postcard to their parents). This part of Springfield Road was badly affected by wartime bombing and all the houses on the left have gone. Also missing is the Co-op store on the corner, built in 1897. Their many shops in Foleshill are a testament to the strength of the Co-operative movement in the area. Today the houses have been replaced by the Polish church and community centre to cater for Poles that settled in Coventry in the immediate post-war period. Some of the houses on the right have survived today but the results of war-time bomb damage can be seen by the newer houses alongside.

Foleshill Road junction with Eagle Street 1906 (E.R.)

The rapid development of lower Foleshill can be judged by a comparison of these two views taken from a similar viewpoint, only six years apart. Both show the Golden Eagle at 178 Foleshill Road on the right. It was opened only a few years earlier in 1903 to serve this rapidly growing area. The pub was built at the junction with Eagle Street which was laid out more than a decade earlier providing a route to Stoney Stanton Road. Housing along the street was gradually built up in stages during the 1890s with the last stretch of terraced homes leading up to Foleshill Road being built at the turn of the century. The origin of the Eagle name is unclear, though the cartographer who drew the 1775 Foleshill Enclosure Map was a Thomas Eagle and a large scale map of the Coventry Canal dating from 1809 was drawn by a J. Eagle. In the later view below a new terrace of houses has been built since 1907 beyond the shops shown in the view above. A close up of one of these houses is shown on page16.They represent the frontage of a large estate that used an area of undeveloped land on the north side of Eagle Street. It stretched up to the middle-class villas of Brooklyn and Bird Grove, taking part of the gardens of both. This land was divided into the new streets of George Eliot, Edmund, Ena, Newland and Thornhill Roads. The large building protruding to the left of the view below is the cycle factory of E. O'Brien Ltd featured on page16.

Foleshill Road junction with Eagle Street c1913 (Waterman)

Godiva Harriers outside the Eagle Inn c1912 (Anon.)

This rather damaged photograph shows a group of Godiva Harriers outside their regular meeting place before the First World War at the Golden Eagle pub. This association between sporting teams and pubs was a very common one in the city where it provided a meeting place, a social space and sometimes even changing facilities. It worked well for the clubs and the landlord benefited from the trade. This was one of a number of bases that Godiva used such as the Sydenham Palace after 1918 until they got their own clubhouse as late as 1984.

Edward O'Brien Ltd, Foleshill Road c1910 (Waterman original - HHT reprint)

Fortunately, this building still exists, with the small addition of air raid shelters on the front. It is a rare survival of the many firms that had outgrown their original bases in central Coventry and moved to Foleshill. Here there was plenty of space to expand. It is one of the few buildings left that can testify to the rapid growth of factories built in lower Foleshill during the Edwardian era. It was home to the Challenge Cycle Company, owned by the O'Brien family. The firm had been founded and built up by Francis O'Brien in the late nineteenth century. Presumably, the Edward name used was in honour of his father who was a London solicitor. Francis died in 1913 and the company continued to be run by the family until the Second World War. The building was still being used for cycle sales into the 1990s.

Brooklyn was one of a group of grand early Victorian villas on the east side of Foleshill Road, near to Cash's Lane, set well back behind their drives (see map right). At that time they would have been surrounded by fields. 'The Hollies' and 'Lebanon Cottage' were on its north side and 'The Grove' and 'Bird Grove', two semi-detached houses to the south (the latter being, at one time, the home of George Eliot – see below). By the time of the map, just before the First World War, the house had been bought by the Girls Friendly Society (GFS) and the urban march of Coventry had reached the gates of Bird Grove, which had been absorbed by George Eliot Road. When this view of Brooklyn was taken its southern boundary had shrunk to the new fence seen on the right. The Grove was in the process of being demolished and Edmund Road was being laid out. Brooklyn was previously the home of the Pridmore's, ribbon manufacturers. Malcolm Pridmore was born in the house in 1869 and fittingly, as mayor of Coventry in 1914, opened the new GFS Lodge. Coventry was desperately in need of respectable accommodation for all the women who were

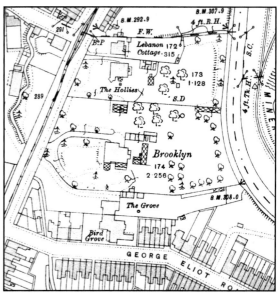

flocking to the city to work in the munitions factories. It offered 36 beds in 12 bedrooms. There was less call for such facilities after the war and by 1933 the building had been replaced by the Redesdale Cinema (later the Roxy). In a sign of the changing social mix in Foleshill, the cinema showed one of the first Asian films in Coventry in 1954. It is fitting that the cinema is still there today as the Sikh Nanaksar Gursikh Temple. Amazingly the two most northerly houses, The Hollies and Lebanon Cottage still survive, albeit in a rather altered state.

BROOKLYN, G.F.S. LODGE, FOLESHILL ROAD, COVENTRY.   *Ward's Studios*

Brooklyn, Foleshill Road c1915 (Ward's Studios)

Bird Grove was the home of author Mary Ann Evans, better known by her pen name of George Eliot. She lived here with her father from 1841-49 after he had retired. It was almost a decade after leaving Bird Grove for London that she had her first novel published. To get a feel for Coventry in the early Victorian period reading George Eliot's *Middlemarch* would be a perfect introduction. This is especially so as the village described as Freshitt in the novel is thought to be Foleshill. A later inhabitant of Bird Grove was Joseph Cash, who with his brother John set up the nearby innovative Kingfield silk weaving factory in 1857. He died

Bird Grove and The Grove c1911 (Waterman)

at Bird Grove in 1880. Although the building was semi-detached the other half known as The Grove was somewhat smaller and was demolished soon after this photograph was taken. This picture, despite the caption given, features mainly the Grove as Bird Grove is to the right partly hidden behind the tree. The building has been owned for many years by the Coventry City Council and has been occupied by a number of tenants. Its future is currently in doubt.

George Eliot Road c1923 (Ralph Athersych)

George Eliot Road had been established just a little over a decade earlier than this photograph. The front gardens were already filling up with plant life. The photographer, Ralph Athersych, lived at the Foleshill Road end of this view, in the distance, just a couple of house from Bird Grove protruding in the centre right of the road. The camera was set up a short distance from where George Eliot Road formed a junction with Leicester Causeway. The woman on the right is in the front garden of number 69. The pillars just beyond led to a large area behind the houses that bordered the Coventry Canal. It was later occupied by the builder J G Gray. Gray was responsible for the development of the nearby Courtaulds factory as well as many other important buildings and housing developments in the city in the early twentieth century. In the year this photograph was taken he bought Coombe Abbey as his home.

210 Foleshill Road was just two houses south of the George Eliot Road junction. Until 1955 it was the home of Minnie Rourke. She can be seen here with the family dog at about the age of sixty. This is a professionally taken photograph, typical of the period, where the house a person lived in had become almost as popular as a subject for the professional photographer as portraiture. The house is shown in its original condition with cast-iron railings and gate. The beautifully finished front door with multi-paned stained glass has been left open but 208, next door, shows what it would have been like. These double bayed houses were a cut above the houses that can be seen in neighbouring George Eliot Road, though built about the same time. Minnie had recently married her husband Richard in 1911 when they were in their 40s. She had run a boarding house in Abbotts Lane and he was a border there. When they moved into 210 it had just been completed in 1912. Richard died in 1939 and Minnie continued to live there until her death in 1955. By 1960 the changing community of Foleshill was reflected in 210's new resident Mr B Singh.

210 Foleshill Road c1920 (Anon.)

Foleshill Road 1906 (E.R.)

To the immediate left of both views is Cash's Lane. The row of cottages opposite the lane is typical of the type that sprung up all over Foleshill in the early nineteenth century as a response to the piecemeal industrial developments in the area. These cottages were not just a rare survival in lower Foleshill, but few of this age were actually built along this part of the road. Most were often associated with small-scale ribbon weaving or, especially in the north of the area, to house coal miners. The second terraced cottage from the right has slightly elongated upper windows to maximise the light, characteristic of those housing simple handlooms. These houses were poorly built and have subsequently been demolished. In the 1860s the toll gate for those entering the Coventry to Leicester turnpike road had been moved to this point from nearer the canal basin. The houses to the left are typical of the early twentieth century suburban development of Foleshill. They were part of the estate of houses created from 1901 between Foleshill Road and the canal made up of Brooklyn Road and Matlock Road. Running through the centre of the estate is Springfield Brook that ends up in the city centre feeding Swanswell Pool. The horse and cart in the view above still delivered the goods for a few more years but would soon be replaced by mechanised transport, first pioneered by a steam tram along the road to Bedworth in the 1880s.

Foleshill Road c1912 (Anon.)

Cash's Lane c1910 (WY)

Long before the changes that the late nineteenth century brought to lower Foleshill, the Cash brothers' 1857 cottage factory was the building that dominated the area. Surrounding the factory was open countryside with a canal snaking through it. The view of the factory above shows the original façade fronting Cash's Lane, just beyond the narrow canal bridge. The bridge was widened in 1912 as shown in the aerial view below and opposite. The view also shows that the original conception of a quadrangle of cottages with their weaving top-shops above was only half completed. The side to the north and that alongside Kingfield Road was not built and the space was later filled with a more conventional factory arrangement. It was the brothers' bad luck that a few years after starting the building in the late 1850s top shop based silk weaving became uneconomic. They converted all the individual attic weaving spaces into one big powered conventional production area. The philanthropic approach of the Quaker Cashs still ensured a dining room, library, workmen's club and cricket ground for their 400 workers, and the fifty cottages for accommodation. The company survived by weaving a variety of specialist delicate woven goods such as name tags for clothes and trimmings for dolls and infants' dresses. These changes introduced had ensured a thriving business for more than a century after the factory was built.

J. & J. CASH Ltd.
KINGFIELD WORKS
COVENTRY, England

Cash's Kingfield Works c1925 (Anon.)

An illustration in the 27 July 1912 edition of the Coventry Graphic showed how the rebuilding of Cash's Bridge was progressing. The buildings in the background are the terrace of houses on Cash's Lane leading back to Foleshill Road. This was a country road (known then as Honey Lane) in 1755 when the canal was built. All that was required then was a simple bridge that could take a horse and cart. By 1912 the increased traffic with heavier vehicles from developments in the Kingfield Road area made the necessity for widening an urgent matter.

Photo by Jackson and Son

The widening of Cash's Bridge.

The Widening of Cash's Bridge 1912 (Coventry Graphic)

Prince William Henry Inn, Foleshill Road 1927 (Anon.)

Apart from the cottages opposite Cash's Lane, virtually the only rural survival in lower Foleshill is the Prince William Henry Inn, which dates from the late eighteenth century. With the canal at its rear and a wharf by Foleshill Road bridge, the canal would have offered some useful additional passing trade. Quite possibly the location of the inn may have been determined by the construction of the canal. It appears that the building may have originally been a row of cottages of which the pub was just a part. The enlarged windows on the left look as if at least one may have been adapted to provide improved lighting for an early weavers loom loft. In 2004 application had been made by the Punch Pub Company to demolish the building, but it was saved by the council. Sadly its façade has been obscured by the hoardings of the building supplies company who now occupy the old pub.

Courtaulds football team outside the Prince William Henry, Foleshill Road 1912 (Jackson & Son)

The big amateur cup final for all Coventry football teams was the Nursing Cup and, as with football today, May was the month for cup finals. As the celebrations indicate, Courtaulds won the final in 1912 against St Michaels. They were known as the 'Silk-Worms' and although most of the team worked at Courtaulds, better players were beginning to be imported from outside the factory. Appropriately their supporters and players celebrated at their local pub after informally parading the cup through the area. The Coventry Graphic of 11 May 1912 (see below) showed some celebrating supporters strung across Foleshill Road.

Courtauld's victory in Foleshill Nursing Cup over St. Michael's.   A few jubilant supporters.   " We all go the same way home."

Photo by Jackson & Son.

Foleshill Vics Football Team, 10 February 1917 (Sylvester)

Like elsewhere in Coventry, Foleshill's football teams started with the introduction of half day working on Saturday's. It had many teams, often based on church groups such as St Paul's (The Saints), works teams like Courtaulds (the Silk-Worms), or simply community teams such as Foleshill Vics who are shown in this wintery scene outside their playing fields pavilion.

2. Middle Foleshill Road: Great Heath, Edgwick and Holbrooks

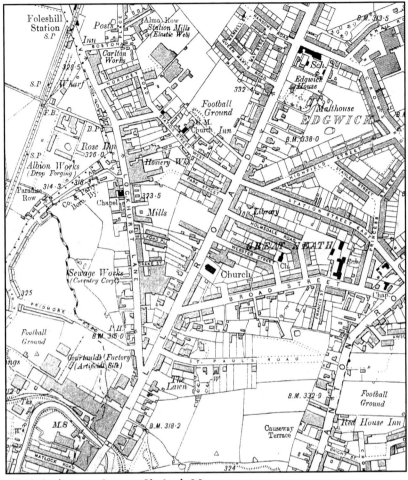

1912 Ordnance Survey Six Inch Map

This section marks the entry into Foleshill proper. In passing Cash's Lane we have also crossed the parish boundary, south of the canal bridge. To old timers, the residents of this area were known as 'people o'er the bridge'. In 1947 the Coventry Evening Telegraph reported the reminiscences of Walter Dunn who could remember the area in Victorian times. *"The present generation will scarcely believe that it was a real old country road with meadows on either side bordered with high hedges and tall trees from Cash's Lane to Little Heath. What a picture in May and June, the hedges covered with hawthorn blossom with the wild rose and honeysuckle and crab apple blossom all along the highway. One could stand at the General Wolfe and look north and south for a straight mile, the entire view being pleasant country"* (Coventry Evening Telegraph 21 August 1947). The mention of the General Wolfe indicates that this area was not quite uninhabited at the time. Indeed the presence of a couple of schools, a church, three chapels, many weaving premises, as well as a couple more pubs indicates a healthy industrial community in the mid-nineteenth century.

The place name Great Heath, and a little further up the road Parting of the Heaths and Little Heath, all give an indication that this area would not have been considered valuable agricultural land, as elsewhere in Foleshill. So when weavers and coalminers began populating Foleshill from the early eighteenth century this area would have been easier for squatter settlements to become established. As a consequence of this population growth, the focus of Foleshill gradually moved from the north of the parish. By 1841 a new church, St Paul's, was built at Great Heath to serve the growing area with a new parish carved out of the southern section of the old parish of Foleshill, centred on the new church.

As with lower Foleshill, major expansion came in the 1890s, soon boosted by the inclusion of this area in Coventry's 1899 boundary extension. Some of the more significant private building developments in the whole of Foleshill happened at this time. For example, the Foleshill Park Building estate on the east side of the road began in the 1890s and the Great Heath Estate, on the west side, from 1912. But there were many other smaller building schemes filling in the spaces flanking the established roads in the area, especially Foleshill Road itself and Lockhurst Lane, but also Broad Street (formerly Brick Kiln Lane) and Station Street West (formerly Carpenters Lane). The creation of new connecting roads such as St Paul's Road and Station Street East offered even more opportunities for residential and commercial building.

Samuel Courtauld Ltd c1910 (Waterman)

From the middle of the eighteenth century, the canal bridge from which this first photograph is taken was considered the entrance to Foleshill. It became a less distinctive landmark after it was widened in 1909. However, in 1905 another landmark in the form of Courtaulds' newly built factory took its place. By the time it closed in the 1990s textile manufacture had moved to the Far East and despite developing new materials such as carbon fibre, it was not enough to keep it open. The first building on the site was not very conspicuous being made up of the single storey building in the foreground of both views. Courtaulds took over the fourteen acre site belonging to Aubrey Seaman & Co, timber merchants who had closed three years earlier. The aim was to use their new invention to mass produce artificial fibres. Initially, there were many technical difficulties but soon the process was perfected and the scale of the operation was greatly extended. It is the later extensions that impressed by their scale, as shown by the view above, but even more so in the view below, with the iconic clock tower. Although today most of the factory has now been demolished the section including the clock tower and some of the associated building beside has been tastefully renovated and now functions as an attractive office block. Its retention was not a certainty at the time the factory was closed but is a tribute to enlightened thinking that such an important building's contribution to Foleshill's heritage has been appreciated.

Samuel Courtauld Ltd c1913 (Waterman)

Samuel Courtauld Ltd c1910 (Waterman)

Why Courtaulds came to Coventry might have been based on a number of factors. The site was convenient being near to the Coventry to Nuneaton railway, and on the tram route between Coventry and Bedworth. It was also beside the Coventry canal that can be seen crossing the centre of the view above up to the canal bridge on Foleshill Road on the far right. The canal was as much used as a water supply as for transporting bulk materials. The factory had plenty of room to expand to the north and the west. By the First World War, they had filled all the area from the canal up to Lockhurst Lane and back to Narrow Lane (now known as Kingfield Road), including a football pitch for their successful football team, the Silk Worms. More women than men were employed at the factory (75% of the workforce was female) and social facilities were also provided for them, including primitive swimming facilities in one of the giant water tanks. Transporting the 3000 workers employed by 1913 was a mammoth task, greatly aided by the tram service, where extra vehicles were deployed at the start and end of the day. The route north to Bedworth was especially useful to draw on the female labour force that was available in the Foleshill district. Women had traditionally taken on paid work, especially in the north of the parish in the silk weaving cottage industry. The decline of silk weaving had created a reservoir of available female labour. This was a useful situation for Courtaulds who had themselves started out as silk weavers in Essex in the late eighteenth century. The view below shows the 1920s view of the factory's later expansion up to the Lockhurst Lane junction with Foleshill Road showing the building as it was to remain for the rest of the twentieth century. The smell associated with the chemical process should not be forgotten and gave rise to a popular ditty; *'Courtaulds built a chimney/It wasn't built for smoke/But to take the stink from Foleshill/And dump it down in Stoke'*!

Courtaulds Ltd c1928 (G & Co)

Lockhurst Lane 1907 (E.R.)

The many changes to the entrance of the old rural Lockhurst Lane from Foleshill Road are represented by these two views. The first shows the buildings by the corner with Foleshill Road and the second is about 100 metres further along. The Stag and Pheasant is common to both views, being just visible half way down the left-hand side of the view above and on the immediate left of the view below. The pub first opened in 1830, which makes it today a very rare survivor of that period in Lockhurst Lane, although in 1907 most other buildings on the west side, leading up to Holbrooks, also dated from that period and many were still occupied by ribbon weavers. The long horizontal window of an early weaving shop can be seen this side of the pub in the above view. Although Clarendon Terrace, on the left was only recently built in 1907, it did not survive the inter-war expansion of Courtaulds factory. Nor did most of the other buildings as far as Kingfield Road (or Narrow Lane as it was then) on the left-hand side of either view

Most of the land to the immediate right through to Foleshill Road was originally occupied by three large houses with open land beyond, but by the beginning of the twentieth century this had partly given way to the terraced housing seen below. However, the back wall of the one surviving property can be seen jutting out on the right of the view below, This was Vauxhall House, described in more detail on page34, where its front wall is shown in Foleshill Road. Twentieth century development has led to Lockhurst Lane road being widened and with it has gone the initiative to establish an avenue of trees to soften the edges of urban growth.

Lockhurst Lane 1907 (E.R.)

Lockhurst Lane 1907 (ER)

The planting of saplings in Lockhurst Lane extended all the way to Foleshill station, which is just behind the photographer in the view above facing east. The terrace to the left, built in 1900, can still be seen today with Northey Road junction on the left, by the lamp post. The collection of old cottages to the right are the remnants of the piecemeal occupation of this area from more than a century before, having more in common with the rural settlements of northern Foleshill hamlets than the Edwardian urban landscape. Most were swept away in a sea of tarmac when the road was widened to accommodate the railway flyover built in 1931.

LEICESTER COUNCILLORS IN COVENTRY.

Municipal Houses Inspected.

LEICESTER AND COVENTRY COUNCILLORS OUTSIDE THE MUNICIPAL HOUSES IN NARROW LANE.

INTERIOR OF ONE OF THE HOUSES.

Coventry is not the only municipality which is suffering from a shortage of houses. There is a similar scarcity of cheap dwellings at Leicester, and with a view to ascertaining the kind of house that had been erected by the Coventry Council, a deputation from Leicester Council visited the city on Saturday and inspected the cottages in Narrow Lane. The above photos were taken during their tour of inspection.

Narrow Lane Council Houses 16 January 1914 (Coventry Graphic)

In 1907 Coventry's first council houses were built in Pridmore Road and Narrow Lane (now Kingfield Road), behind the area of land on the right of the view above. The 48 houses were a breakthrough for those who had been campaigning for more small, cheap accommodation of which there was a scarcity in Coventry. The enormous growth of Coventry's industry during the early years of the century had put an impossible demand on the housing stock. This had given rise to overcrowding in parts of the city. Although there was rapid growth of housing estates around the city suburbs, it was insufficient for the numbers arriving. But even the new houses were too expensive for the poorest paid workers and their families. Coventry City Council's plan was for more than 200 houses in Narrow Lane and in new streets to be laid out alongside. The full plan was not enacted until 1912 when houses began to be built in what were named Pridmore Road, Guild Road and Maycock Road. The even more rapid expansion of the city during the First World War meant that other council homes were soon to be added to the Council's stock in the Stoke Heath and Charterhouse estates.

W J Stafford, Baker, 146 Lockhurst Lane c1910 (Anon.)

These two bakers, a quarter of a century apart, used quite different forms of transport. Stafford's horse and trap had been about for centuries whereas Frisby's electric van was quite advanced even by today's standards. Stafford's shop was just north of the Livingstone Road junction with Lockhurst Lane and continued in business until just before the Second World War after almost a hundred years in business. Frisby's van was a Morrison's Electric 'Terrier' which was made in Leicester. It had a range of 30 miles, which like later milk floats would be perfectly adequate for a daily round of customers' deliveries. The horse and trap would do a similar job but needed accommodation for the horse and more time-consuming upkeep. The provision of a bakery round like many other home delivery services has become rarer with the convenience of the supermarket shop. Frisby's house is still standing but Stafford's shop, just north of Livingstone Road, did not survive the immediate post-war period.

W F Frisby, Baker, 54 Durbar Avenue c1935 (Frisby)

Lockhurst Lane Bridge c1935 (Valentine)

When the railway line between Coventry and Nuneaton opened in 1851 it cut across a number of roads without building bridges under or over them. Lockhurst Lane was a quiet country road so even a level crossing was not provided. This continued to be the case for another sixty years until more factories, and therefore workers came to this part of Foleshill. The problem was particularly pronounced during the First World War when the White and Poppe munitions factory in Holbrooks expanded to employ many thousands of workers. At the beginning and the end of the working day there was chaos with workers arriving and departing by tram and train and queues building up either side of the level crossing. A footbridge was the first solution but that did not solve the problem of congestion created by road transport. The situation became so bad that a flyover was considered the only viable solution. It was to be more than a decade later that it opened in 1931 at a cost of £55,000, providing essential relief that continues today. As the view below shows it did prove a problem to the shops that had become established on the Holbrooks side of the bridge and so their frontages needed to be revised to take account of the new gradient. The Railway Hotel on the town side of the bridge had the buffer of a side road to protect its frontage.

New Bridge, Lockhurst Lane 1931 (Teesee)

White & Poppe, Lockhurst Lane, Holbrooks, Foleshill

(i) Whitmore Park Hostels c1916 (Anon.)

(ii) Munition Workers, Holbrook Lane 1918 (Anon.)

(iii) Queen Mary's visit 18 September 1917 (Curtis)

(iv) 'Announcing the" Ceasefire!" at White and Poppe's Ltd and National Filling Factory, Coventry 11 November 1918'

Although established in 1899 and operating in Coventry until 1933, White and Poppe's history will always be defined by what it achieved during the First World War. It grew steadily in its early years as an engine manufacturer located in Lockhurst Lane. Its premises expanded along with its success, south of Drake Street until a large new factory was built on the site in 1912. However, it was with the outbreak of war and the development of a 141 acre new factory just beyond the level crossing in Holbrooks Lane, when the business really took off. At the start of the War they employed 350 people and by the end it was nearer 12,000. As well as engines they produced many sorts of munitions, employing many women from all over Britain (the famed 'canary girls'). To house them huts were built in the vicinity of the factory as vast hostels. Many were still being used in the 1930s to house local families. Such was the firm's achievements that Queen Mary and Princess Mary visited in 1917. White & Poppe did not adjust well to peacetime and its factory was shared with other manufacturers such as Dunlop, The Standard Motor Co. and eventually by Swallow, Sidecars Co., later to become Jaguar.

Announcing the "Cease Fire!" at White & Poppe's Ltd and National Filling Factory, Coventry. Nov 11. 1918.

Photo.
Bradbury
Stockingford.

Foleshill Park (Holbrooks Park), Holbrooks Lane c1928 (G & Co)

By the time the above view was published Holbrooks had developed its own distinct identity, but perversely it was called Foleshill Park and did not become Holbrooks Park until the latter part of the twentieth century. Up to the end of the nineteenth century, and beyond, much of Holbrooks was within the parish of Foleshill, including Holbrooks Lane. It is then rather ironic to find that Foleshill Park was in fact even outside this boundary, so definitely never part of Foleshill parish. The boundary ran down the centre of Holbrooks Lane and Foleshill Park is west of that boundary. A park was considered necessary because of the growing population in the area and in 1914 the city council proposed to buy 22 acres of land for £3700 opposite St Paul's cemetery. A park keeper was appointed, shown here, who locked the iron gates at dusk. The gates and railings were scrapped for the war effort and never replaced. Also removed was a trophy field gun from the First World War, displayed in the background; a common practice after the War.

In the view below Foleshill parish embraces both sides of the road. Holbrooks' housing estates first developed in the late 1920s and early 1930 as part of the Whitmore Park Estate. This point in Holbrooks Lane is where Park Gate Road joins it, just beyond the van on the left. Whitmore Park Road post office can be seen on the right-hand side with the Lyric cinema beyond. There had been a smaller cinema here opened in 1927 as the Corona, accommodating an audience of less than 400. By 1931 it was known as the Lyric and in 1937 it was rebuilt to seat more than 800. It eventually closed in 1968 and became a bingo hall, which itself closed in 1990 and is now a retail outlet.

Lyric Cinema, Holbrooks Lane c1938 (Richards)

Unveiling the Foleshill War Memorial, Durbar Avenue 1919 (Sylvester)

The First World War was commemorated in a number of ways by different communities across Coventry. Both Foleshill and Earlsdon erected full sized memorials in wood and plaster that they hoped to replace with permanent versions in stone. In neither case did this happen. The view above shares another thing in common with Earlsdon which is the planned development of a large estate by the Newcombe brothers of Market Harborough. They had already built the infrastructure for housing estates between Albany Road and Hearsall Common in Earlsdon and were now planning to develop the land between Lockhurst Lane, Station Street West and Foleshill Road up to the Coventry Loop Line, as shown in the plan below. The Coventry Graphic in May 1912 suggested that 1200 houses were planned. Although they had bought the land before the First World War restrictions on the use of construction materials meant few houses were built until after 1918. So the sign, enlarged from the main photograph that stood in front of Foleshill railway station is still advertising the land 'to be sold in lots'. T D Griffiths drew up the plans for all their Coventry schemes, including the one here. Typically the brothers never built houses, only laid out the services and the building plots. A builder would decide how many plots they wanted to buy and from then on they would be responsible for construction and sale. Although there would be some latitude for a builder to introduce slightly different styles of façade and room layout, building line and general appearance was laid down by the Newcombe Brothers. Also, they would not allow public houses or chip shops on their estates, the former partly explained by their non-conformist beliefs.

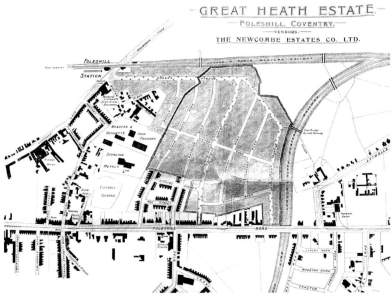

Plan of the Great Heath Estate 1912 (T.D. Griffiths)
(See inside front cover for a larger view)

Foleshill Gymnastic Club, Northey Road c1935 (Anon.)

This fine body of men makes up the membership of the Foleshill Gymnastic Club, founded in 1929. The individual kneeling on the far left is John Walmsley who was the leading light of the club, being the 'Chief Instructor and Masseur'. In a notebook for the club he was described as being ten stones in weight and 5ft 6ins in height and an amateur strongman known as Young Atlas. He is also shown in the photograph below right, demonstrating the breaking of the chain around his chest, just one of his many feats of strength. The members would meet four days a week, both lunchtime and evenings. The facilities were available for six pence a week which promised *'Perfect Health, Super Strength, Cat-like Agility'*. Below left J Duff is having his three monthly checks on his height and weight; this was a rule of the club to ensure progress was

being made. Note the sign behind him for refreshments at their bar, e.g. Tea, Bovril, Cocoa, Oxo but no alcohol. All of these fit in with a healthy regime but was also part of the spiritual beliefs of the non-conformist community that was so strong in this district. Whilst body-building and weightlifting featured heavily in their activities boxing, wrestling and fencing were also included. They also visited local events putting on demonstrations of weight-lifting, wrestling and muscle control. At the Walsgrave Fete Young Atlas performed the 'Turkish Strangle', breaking his own record for six men, three a side, pulling on a rope around his neck for 25 seconds!

Foleshill Road c1913 (Waterman)

Just north of the junction of Lockhurst Lane with Foleshill Road there were a number of large houses built in the mid to late Victorian period on both sides of the road. At the time of their construction this part of Foleshill was considered a pleasant rural suburb for the middle classes who wanted to escape Coventry. They were beginning to be surrounded by semi and terraced housing. Some of the former owners were leaving such as in Vauxhall House behind the wall to the left, its grounds reaching through to Lockhurst Lane. By 1913 it was occupied by the Vauxhall House Working Men's Club and Institute, which itself was demolished to and they moved to new premises in Eld Road. A little further up was Heath House, opposite Broad Street which was still occupied by William Grant a Foleshill resident all his life who, despite his humble origins, became one of the largest Coventry silk ribbon manufacturers. He succeeded the previous owner Eli Green who was as famous as the Cash brothers for his innovative Vernon Street Triangle weaving factory in Hillfields. One of the last of the grand houses to be built was Great Heath House occupied by Dr John Orton. It is just beyond the man with the handcart on the left of the view below, hidden behind later housing and a high wall. Both Grant and Orton were civic minded and represented Foleshill on the City Council; indeed, Grant was Mayor of Coventry in1920 and 1921. Some detached houses, though smaller, were still being built in St Paul's Road a new street on the right, created in the late 1890s, known locally as 'Nobs Row'. But the dominance of lower cost housing had been achieved by the end of the First World War and few larger houses were built in the area after this date. The congregation at St Paul's church, to the right of both views, was greatly swelled by these changes.

Foleshill Road c1913 (Waterman)

Broad Street c1913 (Waterman)

Give Broad Street back its original name of Brick Kiln Lane and its pre-industrial past becomes clear. Much of the south side (on the right of this view from Foleshill Road junction) was already partially occupied by the late eighteenth century with a variety of buildings, including a Workhouse. Before the canal got in the way it was a useful route to the east, across the Stoney Stanton Road and Crabmill Lane to Wyken and Stoke. In the late 1890s the Broad Brothers, John and Edmund, moved to the area from Burslem, Staffordshire and set about building houses along the undeveloped north side of the lane. After 1899, when this part of Foleshill was incorporated into Coventry, to avoid duplication it was renamed Broad Street in honour of the Broad brothers. John died in 1905 but his brother continued to build houses around Coventry into the inter-war years, including Edmund Road, developed in the grounds of Brooklyn opposite Cash's Lane. He lived at Stafford House, 411 Foleshill Road just south of this junction. As in a number of other newly developed streets of this period, trees were planted along the road to soften the landscape, but only a couple have survived at this end of the street. Fortunately, more can be found for most of its length up to the Stoney Stanton Road. Prominent in this view on the right is the Foleshill Spiritual Church which was opened in 1907, but the congregation had first worshipped in the area in 1880.

Another centre of worship was the Wesleyan Chapel at the Stoney Stanton end of Broad Street. It had been established fifty years before the Spiritualists in the 1830s. The chapel was destroyed in the Second World War and its congregation joined the nearby Paradise Chapel. Bands were formed by many organisations in this period, and in this case would help to propagate the message of staying off the demon drink. The band is at the back of the church looking across to the far end of Station Street East.

Broad Street Wesleyan Band 1910 (Anon.)

Ivor Preece, Schoolboy International 1935 (Anon.)
Broad Street School Rugby Team 1937 (Anon.)
Broad Street Orchestra c1912 (Anon.)

Rugby was traditionally a middle-class game, but Coventry's council schools developed a fine reputation for producing many excellent players, a notably large number of whom went on to international honours. Although most of these schools no longer exist their names live on today in the old boys' clubs that developed from these early origins. Broad Street is one of the better known ones. Here is the school team of 1937. On the left is Harold 'Pop' Suddens, sports master. In 1931 he became headmaster, and later President of Coventry Rugby Football Club. On the right is Harold Wapples the teacher in charge of rugby. Two years earlier Ivor Preece was a pupil, shown right in his England schoolboys strip. He not only captained the schoolboys at the national level but also became captain of the full England team and played for the British Lions. In 1929 Foleshill schools were reorganised and most only taught those up to eleven years of age. They then went to Broad Street which had become a secondary school providing the focus for sporting excellence. It was originally opened in 1911 as a mixed boys and girls school. Cultural pursuits were not ignored in this earlier period as is shown in the group photograph of the school orchestra. Broad Street became Broad Heath School in 1949.

Although Foleshill had been served by a parish church for many centuries it was a few miles north of Great Heath. In the gap caused by the neglect by the Church of England in this area, a number of non-conformist chapels had become established and filled the demand for places of worship. Belatedly, the Church of England addressed this problem with the opening of St Paul's in 1841 and the creation of a new parish taken out of the southern part of the old parish. All went well with the church for almost a century until 1940 when it was bombed. Two years later the adjoining Sunday school was destroyed. After some time spent planning, the rebuilding of the church started in 1950 and it formally reopened in 1956.

The architects' model below gives an indication of some of the changes that were made, the most obvious being the reduction of the tower. The external ornamentation was simplified with the omission of the finials on the tower and the rear pediment. There was no clock provided for the locals, although the need would not be as great as it had been in the mid-nineteenth century. Additional community facilities were provided at the rear. The original churchyard was surprisingly small given the easy availability of land when it was first laid out, leaving a relatively small amount of space for burials. This was an even greater omission when the size of the church is considered as it had a capacity for more than a thousand worshipers. The photograph above captures the moment when the rural setting of the church with its grass verges was being replaced with pavements and kerbing, though the contemporary popularity of planting roadside saplings softens this process.

St Paul's Church 1906 (E.R.)

War Damage Reinstatement St Paul's Church, model by Nicholson & Rushton c1945 (Anon.)

Park Street 1906 (E.R.)

It is difficult to know how Park Street got its name, as at no time does there appear to have been a park located nearby. Perhaps it was a sales affectation by the developer or maybe it was the football ground immediately to the south which gave it its name. It was one of Foleshill's earliest housing developments with terraces on the right-hand side dating back to the 1880s. When first built it was a cul-de-sac, bordering on the grounds of the ribbon weaving factory of Foleshill Mills, on Lockhurst Lane. The back entrance to this building is shown in the foreground. In the distance are the houses flanking Foleshill Road. The little girl is Nellie Heatley, near her house at 33 Park Street.

Foleshill Road 1906 (E.R.)

This view is taken from the junctions of Station Road East and Station Road West, looking south with St Paul's in the distance on the left. Park Street is a few houses down on the right. It provides yet more evidence of the rapid growth of this part of Foleshill in the previous decade. A few of the houses had been planned from the start as shops but others were later converted into shop frontages from domestic dwellings. The more radical changes were yet to come as even the London, City & Midland Bank Ltd premises on the far left were quite restrained. Only the new General Wolfe, rebuilt in the mid-1890s, was on a much larger scale. Contrast this with the development shown six years later in the views opposite, in which the area has taken on the appearance of a small town centre.

Foleshill Road c1913 (Waterman)

In these two north facing views the photographer has captured the section of Foleshill Road that represents the recently evolved shopping centre at Great Heath; it remains the commercial heart of the area today. They give a good feel for how important this area had become as a commercial focus for the growing local population. It provides an interesting contrast with the rather more limited development shown on the previous page, only six years earlier. Two banks had now opened branches here. But even more significant is the bright white façade of one of Coventry's first cinemas, the Grand Picture Theatre, opened two years earlier in 1911. Here we see the cinema in its original form, housing an audience of 450. In 1927 it was enlarged to accommodate 900 and its façade was changed. Inset is the same view, taken at the same time, from the opposite direction with the cinema in the distance.

In the view below Holmesdale Road is to the immediate right and the large Co-op store on its corner had only opened a couple of years earlier in 1908. It was a branch of the Lockhurst Lane Co-op that claimed to be one of the oldest in the country, hence the "Estd. 1832" claim above the entrance. The building still exists today with its decorative brickwork plastered over and minus its pinnacles. In the middle distance on the left can be seen the General Wolfe, originally a small eighteenth-century country pub, like the Prince William Henry, until the mid-1890s when it was rebuilt in the grand style it retains today, albeit no longer a pub.

Foleshill Road c1913 (Waterman)

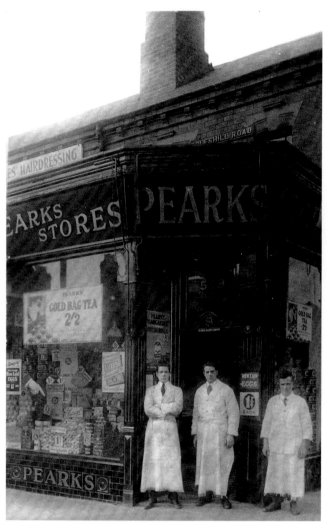

Here is a useful case study of how the face of Foleshill was being changed in the Great Heath area. The original house was part of a terrace of houses that was built in the late 1890s on the corner of Station Street West. The building was typical of many Foleshill shops, being an afterthought rather than a purpose built property. As the area became more populated shop conversions were common and as business improved they expanded their shop frontages into the front gardens. Gradually the neighbours joined in this process and a residential terrace was transformed into a shopping parade. This practice can be seen in many other areas of Coventry such as Earlsdon Street where Pearks opened another branch of their business at the corner of Providence Street. Originally a confectionery shop in 1901 and then a grocer in 1903, it was taken over by Pearks in the late 1920s.

The view below is taken from half-way along Station Street West looking towards Foleshill Road. Station Street West takes a dog-leg to the right of the photographer and the 'new' (1900) Northey Road continues behind him. The shop on the left is on the corner of Boyes' Yard, a small cul-de-sac. Numbered 80 Station Street West, it was an off-licence run by Edwin Newman, part of a terrace built just a few years before. The houses on the right were built much earlier as part of an early to mid-nineteenth century weaving community when this long-established route was known as Carpenters Lane. A later top-shop can be seen at right angles to the street at the end of this terrace. A few of the occupants were still working in that industry when this photograph was taken. In the distance, the early twentieth century terraces can be seen that filled the gaps left in the street. Roadworks on the right are laying out paving stones for a pavement

Pearks Grocers, 549 Foleshill Road c1930 (Anon.)

as part of the latest improvements brought by the development of this area. Twenty years earlier gas lamps were installed in the lane, one of which can be seen on the left.

Station Street West (Carpenters Lane) 1906 (E.R.)

PLAN OF
FOLESHILL PARK BUILDING ESTATE,
1891.

— SCALE 66 FEET TO AN INCH —

Plan of Foleshill Park Building Estate 1891 (Coventry Archives PA279/4/53)

The Foleshill Park Estate was the first large residential estate to be developed in Foleshill. The developers had bought three fields between Foleshill Road and Stoney Stanton Road. In 1891 they publicised their plan to fill the fields with four roads containing 163 plots for sale to builders. The initial sales publicity from 1891 claimed the houses were to be *'of a small type intended to be for mechanics and artisans'*. The roads were named Highfield Street, Stanley Street, Victory Street and Station Road East. Only the latter retained its original name, the others were changed to Eld, Road, St Elizabeth's Road and Princess Streets respectively in the 1930s. Station Street East was officially taken over by the council in 1893. The photograph shown faces east, near the junction with Foleshill Road. Highfield Street is the first road on the left. These earliest residential estates in Foleshill look to be spaciously designed and with the trees flanking the road they make the estate look quite attractive as the view suggests. Unfortunately today, with cars parked in the street they are rather congested. It is some compensation that the rear gardens are large by comparison with modern developments.

Station Street East c1913 (Waterman)

Highfield Street (later Eld Road) 1906 (E.R.)

Apart from Station Street East Highfield Street was the most rapidly developed part of the Foleshill Park Estate. But even after fifteen years or so, many building plots throughout the estate remained undeveloped. The houses in Highfield Street, as shown in this view, only reached as far as the site of the later church. Like the trees in Station Street East, those here have not survived into the twenty-first century, but some maintenance had been taken in the early years of their life as they have been pollarded. The washing dollys outside the shop on the left, at the corner with Station Street East, show how clothes were hand washed in a tub before the washing machine age.

In 1912 a number of vacant plots on the corner of Stanley Road and Highfield Road were bought as the site for a Roman Catholic Church. A growing Catholic population had led to a demand for the first suburban Catholic church in Coventry. Masses were first held in a hall on the site and then in 1916 the church shown below of the Good Shepherd and St Elizabeth and St Helen was opened. St Elizabeth's was damaged in a 1941 air raid in the subsequent rebuild the opportunity taken to extend and accommodate an additional 150 worshippers on top of the original 450. The restored church was opened in 1962 has taken its design cues from the original. In the same year that the original church was opened, St Elizabeth's Roman Catholic School was opened on the site. Over the course of the next century the school has taken over the land behind the building up to Princess Street, partly facilitated by the post-war demolition of a row of terraced houses on the south side of St Elizabeth's Road.

St Elizabeth's Church, Highfield Street (later Eld Road) c1925

This rather faded photograph is a rare survival of the tragic events of Saturday 9 July 1910. Viola Spencer (real name Edith Cooke) was an exceptionally adventurous woman and a survivor of more than 300 parachute descents. She would hang onto a trapeze bar attached to the parachute and then be released from a balloon after it had reached a few thousand feet. She is shown here holding onto the apparatus that is attached to the balloon at the Lilywhite Fete held at the Angel sports ground near the General Wolfe. She was a last minute stand-in for the previously booked Dolly Shepherd. All went well to begin with after the balloon took off. She released the parachute but was then caught by a change in wind and drifted towards Coventry collided with the roof of the Market Hall and then onto the roof of the Centaur Cycle Works in West Orchard. She fell to the ground breaking her pelvis and arm. Despite being rushed to hospital she died of her injuries a few days later. Viola's aerial activities since 1898 had been quite remarkable irrespective of her gender. They included learning to fly in France, becoming arguably the world's first female pilot and certainly the first British woman to pilot a plane.

Miss Viola Spencer, balloonist and parachutist at the Lillywhite's Fete 1910 (Maule & Co)

Athletics Meeting at the Angel Sports Ground 30 March 1929 (Anon.)

This was a meeting organised by the Coventry branch of the Birchfield Harriers at the Angel Sports ground. Here we see those who were awarded prizes for the 220 yards Ladies Open Handicap. In the centre is V Keeling of Birchfield Harriers who came first, on the left W Attwood of Birchfield Harriers, second and on the right N Hopkins of Nelson Harriers who came third. The Angel was an old Foleshill pub set back from Station Street West only a short distance from the General Wolfe. It closed the public in the 1980s, but for many years had the special attraction of having a sports ground on its doorstep. In 1936 it was sold for housing and Blackwell Road was built over it.

Edgewick Infants School, Cross Road c1910 (Anon.)

Following the passing of the 1870 Education Act school boards were set up across England to ensure an education for all. One was made responsible for the Foleshill area. Edgewick School (the school still uses one of the old spellings for the district) in Cross Road was the first to be opened under this new body in 1876, followed by Foxford School in 1877. The school, on the corner of Cross Road and Foleshill Road, was rebuilt in the 1970s, and that was replaced by a complete rebuild in 2016 which has doubled its capacity. The facilities today would be unimaginable to these pupils who would have worn their best clothes, such as they were, for the visit of the photographer.

Foleshill Wedding c1925 (E M Turner)

Edith Mary Turner established her photographic studio in 1921 at 431 Foleshill Road, opposite the Broad Street junction. Despite the first photographic businesses having been established in Coventry more than sixty years earlier, Turner was the first woman to be recorded as owning a studio. This outdoor wedding group would have been one of her early commissions. Turner stayed in business for another decade before her studio was taken over by P. O. McNamara. He only stayed for a few years before it fell into the hands of H. G. Coomber, also organist at the Broad Lane Methodist Chapel. He was still in business after the War.

3. Upper Foleshill Road:
Parting of the Heaths and Little Heath

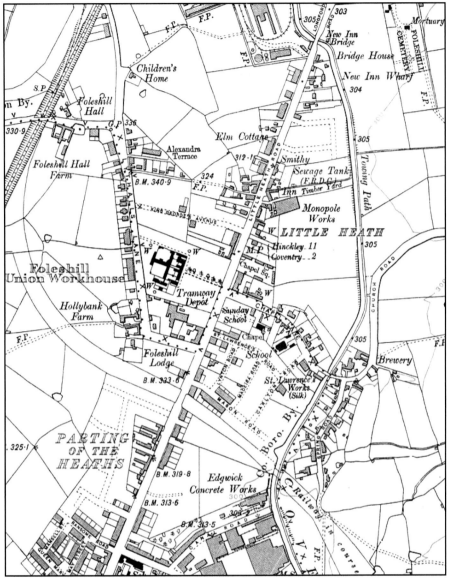

1912 Ordnance Survey Six Inch Map

This is a particularly complex area of Foleshill to unravel. It is clear from the place names how the underlying historic landscape might have appeared. Having just left the 'Great Heath' area we then enter the 'Little Heath' area, but not before passing through the 'Parting of the Heaths'. It is not necessary to wrestle with the Anglo Saxon language to work out what is going on, but the lack of ancient place names may indicate how relatively late this area was settled. The Foleshill enclosure map of the eighteenth century gives some clues about the evolution of the use of land in the parish. It appears that roughly a third of the land had been traditionally farmed in strips in the open fields, mainly to the west of Little Heath. Another third was farmed in ancient enclosed fields that had been carved out of uncultivated land over the centuries which tended to be on the western, northern and eastern edges of the parish. The final third was common, uncultivated land or 'waste'. Heathland would be included in this last category and was largely to the south of Little Heath.

During the nineteenth century much of Foleshill Road was still surrounded by fields rather than buildings, the only exceptions being a group of weavers' cottages and a pub on the west side of the road at the Parting of the Heaths, and a larger settlement at Little Heath. Most groups of cottages were found off the main road in the old side lanes such as Lythalls Lane, Chapel Lane (Old Church Road) and Spring Road. Spring Road was an old route to the east before the construction of the canal made it into a no through road.

Sadly, few of the buildings that made up the nineteenth century settlements in this area still survive in their original state, to give testimony to the former streetscape. From 1925 the whole area east of Foleshill Road and north of Chapel Lane was gradually cleared for the Courtaulds Factory. It was later known as British Celanese. The area is now been redeveloped for the typical Foleshill mix of residential and industrial. Important public buildings such as the Foleshill Workhouse the Tramway Depot and some of the original school buildings have also gone.

Just like the Coventry Canal before it, the creation of the Coventry Loop Line (also known as the Gosford Spur) railway in 1914 influenced the urban shape of the area as the route of the track restricted the flow of development. This is even more the case today as the old line, closed in 1981, has been converted into the A444 dual carriageway, creating an even larger barrier.

Silk Ribbon Weaving in the Foleshill District

The late Harry Laxon, of Coventry, and his Working Model of a Silk Ribbon Weaving Loom.

Harry Laxon's Working Model of a Silk Ribbon Weaving Loom 1912 (J T Hall)

Laxon's model shows an engine loom where more than one ribbon can be woven at a time. It could be converted to use by steam power by using the pulley seen at the back of the machine. Harry worked his whole life as a handloom weaver, as his father had, both living in Whitefriars Street. The fact that he continued to work as a ribbon weaver into the twentieth century, almost half a century after the collapse of the industry showed the resilience of the trade in some areas of Coventry, including Foleshill.

The importance of the weaving industry to the Foleshill area influenced the lives of the inhabitants for almost two hundred years and as such is deserving of a more detailed description. Fortunately, we know a little about the operation of the industry and its impact on the area from a couple of Royal Commission investigations into handloom weaving. They visited the Coventry area during the first half of the nineteenth century. The more the topic is explored the more complicated it becomes. For instance; if the industry collapsed in 1860 because it became uneconomic why were there still weavers working at home in the late 1930s and new weaving factories being built after 1860? How was it possible to have so many people working in the weaving industry yet so little evidence of it today?

Silk weaving had become established in Coventry in the early eighteenth century by a Mr Bird, supposedly with the help of French Huguenots who had brought their expertise with them when they fled persecution in France in the late seventeenth century. Most weaving at this time was done on a single hand loom with which an operator would weave one ribbon at a time. This would not require much space and could be simply accommodated in any ordinary Coventry town hovel or Foleshill cottage. But weavers needed to be provided with work by the middlemen who distributed the material. Coventry weavers were always the first in the queue and those in the countryside would only be given work if there was too much for the city, so they tended to be unemployed more often and on lower rates of pay. In the late eighteenth century the engine loom, also known as the Dutch loom, was introduced to Coventry. It could weave more than one ribbon at a time. Despite its name, it was also hand operated. The discrepancy between Foleshill and Coventry was emphasised by the fact that in 1818 there were only 110 engine looms in Foleshill but 2,259 in Coventry. Conversely, there were 1,008 single hand-looms in Coventry but 1,622 in Foleshill. This pattern of being the poor cousin to Coventry continued through the nineteenth century. For the simple handloom weavers of Foleshill it was mainly a trade dominated by women, with husbands working in mines or agriculture. The opposite applied in Coventry where women were effectively banned from using the more productive looms. Operating an engine loom could bring in a good living for a male operator. A single loom operator did have one advantage over the engine loom, if they were sufficiently skilled, as engine looms could only produce relatively narrow plain ribbons, but a hand loom was capable of wider strips and ones that could be patterned.

In the early 1820s, a new machine was introduced that would influence the architecture of weavers top-shops. The Jacquard loom could weave multiple ribbons that were patterned (See The Herbert Museum's 1845 example right). The only problem, apart from its expense, was its size as its complicated mechanism needed to be added to the top of an engine loom which meant that new top shops had to be made with a taller room for the loom or older top-shops needed remodelling. A mini-boom in the building of new top shops was reported in Foleshill in the late 1820s and by 1838 400 Jacquard looms had been installed in the area whilst the number of engine looms declined. It should be noted that the Foleshill total was still dwarfed by the 1,278 Jacquard looms in Coventry. Added to this development was the introduction of steam power to the larger looms in the 1830s. Examples of these buildings can be seen in the photographs opposite of the top-shops in Parting of the Heaths. However, throughout this period the majority of Foleshill weavers still operated single handlooms and engine looms and continued to do so into the twentieth century. It was a very insecure trade and there were frequent periods of unemployment and poverty was rife. Weavers were regularly admitted to the Foleshill Workhouse and the area had a bad reputation for lawlessness, and stealing from the canal barges was a common occurrence especially in the early to

Wilkinson's Jaquard ribbon weaving loom 1845 (Herbert Art Gallery & Museum)

Grants Factory, Lockhurst Lane 17 August 1918 (Coventry Graphic)

mid-nineteenth century.

Although the single hand loom had the handicap of being a slow method it was flexible and allowed the weaver to adapt to new materials. Weavers now turned their hand to elastic webbing and various trimmings as did Foleshill manufacturers such as Cash's and Pridmore's (later Grant's), offering a lifeline to the self-employed and others in the industry when silk weaving offered such low returns after 1860. At least it offered the opportunity for earning some money during the frequent spells of poor opportunities of alternative employment. Nevertheless, there were times in the 1870s when silk weaving had a resurgence, but it did not last for long and by 1890 employment was every bit as bad as in the 1860s. But by then more alternative factory work had begun to move to the area.

Grant's silk ribbon factory was still going strong in 1918. It adapted the Jacquard technology to produce woven pictures, bookmarks, postcards etc. The charabancs shown here were to take the factory workers on a day trip to Knowle. Note the original mid-nineteenth top-shops fronting the Livingstone Mills factory. It was all destroyed in the Blitz.

Parting of the Heaths, Foleshill Road 1906 (E.R.)

This scene is unusual as it features a cluster of different ribbon weavers' top-shops which, outside of Hillfields, were rarely found in large groups such as this and may be the only ones that fronted Foleshill Road. Although a few could also be found in some of the small lanes off Foleshill Road (see other pages for Harnall Lane West and Hurst Lane, for example), only Stoney Stanton Road featured significant numbers in the area. This group is also remarkable for rather special building on the left. The height of its loom loft and the decorative use of bricks are exceptional for any anywhere in Coventry. Like some of the other less striking top-shops further up the road, their large loom lofts would have been built to take the Jacquard looms that had been recently introduced in the 1820s. They would also have been steam powered with the engine house out the back, all of which implies a date of construction of about the late 1830s to 1840s. A will of 1854, left by Charles Cross, a ribbon manufacturer of Foleshill (his name is remembered in Cross Road), refers to four buildings and an engine house at Parting of the Heaths which was leased to a John Averns, and describes one of these sets of top-shops, though which one is not clear (Coventry Archives PA 101/7/80). Today the location can be found between Churchill Avenue and where Phoenix Way cuts through Foleshill Road. Only two of the top-shops still exist hidden behind the much-altered façade of two retail outlets south of what was the Heath Hotel (originally the Bricklayers Arms) and is now a nursery. The Foleshill Community Centre occupies the site in the foreground. Appropriately, the significance of the ribbon weaving industry to Foleshill's past has been recognised in the piece of bold artwork displayed on the nearby Phoenix Way traffic island.

The rear of 791-797 Foleshill Road, 1963 (Coventry City Planning Department Archive)

This terrace of four top-shops was part of the far group shown in the photograph on the previous page. They were attached to the only two top-shops that still exist, shown on the far left above. Their generally decrepit state reflects the fate of most other top-shops that had survived into the second half of the twentieth century, and would also be demolished. The rear extensions on the right were found behind a few of the other top-shops in the Parting of the Heaths. They would have accommodated four weaver families, and to judge from the size of the bay window sections, they will probably have housed the tall Jacquard weaving looms on their ground floor, stretching into the second floor. They would also have benefited from the same engine house that also drove the three-storey buildings facing Foleshill Road, improving the overall efficiency of the building's operation and explaining why this configuration was found elsewhere in the Foleshill area.

Foleshill Road 1906 (E.R.)

This photograph of Foleshill is a few hundred metres north of the previous view, with Lythalls Lane in front the buildings with an X marked by the sender (who is boasting of their recently built house). The Coventry Loop Line was built a few years later in 1914 and the bridge to take Foleshill Road was located immediately beside where the photographer was standing. Eighty years on and Phoenix Way was built on the line of the old railway and in laying out the roundabout at this point the houses on the left were demolished. The large house on the corner of Lythalls Lane, behind the tram post on the left, had been a doctor's surgery for much of the twentieth century. The tram in the distance would have been opposite the Foleshill Workhouse on the left with Chapel Lane on the right.

Chapel Lane (Old Church Road), Little Heath 1906 (E.R.)

Today known as Old Church Road, this first stretch of the road from Foleshill Road up to the canal was originally named Chapel Lane as it included the local Congregational Chapel. Built in 1795 it was the oldest non-conformist chapel standing in the Coventry area in the second half of the twentieth century. It has now been demolished and a small housing development, Albert Fearn Gardens built in its place. Alongside the chapel was the Sunday School that still exists, dating from 1848. This group of buildings would have been to the right of the photographer. In the distance the road bends to the right until it reaches Little Heath canal bridge. At the time of the photograph, it then changed from Chapel Lane to Church Road. Eventually, the whole stretch between Foleshill Road and Bell Green became known as Old Church Road. The cottages on the left, Staffords Row, were demolished soon after the First World War. Courtaulds were eventually to dominate the whole of the area north of this view with their 40 acre Little Heath Rayon Works. It opened in 1927 but was demolished in 2009.

Photos by Whitehouse and Thomas.

Snapshots at a recent fire in Chapel Lane, Foleshill.

Fire at Kelly & Sons Timber Yard, Chapel Lane (Old Church Road), 13 June 1913, Coventry Graphic

There were already a couple of works premises in Chapel Lane before the arrival of Courtaulds, most notably Foleshill's only brewery. The Rock Brewery was located behind the Royal Hotel and had been producing beer from the 1880s with outlets in towns all around Coventry. It was still producing beer at the time of the First World War and by then had the mineral water factory of R White & Sons alongside! This interesting pairing did not last long and the brewery site was taken over by their neighbour. On the opposite side of the road just before the canal bridge was the timber yard of Kelly and Sons. There were not infrequent reports of fires in the various timber yards in Coventry and this one at Kelly's premises offered up a couple of dramatic pictures that featured in the weekly Coventry Graphic, but was hardly worthy of a mention in the daily papers who were still coming to terms with incorporating pictures into their production at short notice.

National Union of Ex-Servicemen c1925 (Anon.)

Coventry had been a hotbed of working-class politics since before the First World War with strong trade unions and relatively strong support for the infant Labour Party. Four Labour councillors had been elected in the city in 1913. There was even a Labour MP elected in 1923 and 1929. Foleshill had its fair share of working-class political organisations. The National Union of Ex-Servicemen was one of a number of such organisations which had sprung up after the end of the War to give expression to the concerns of insecure employment that faced the demobbed soldiers. The picture shows a group off on a money collecting expedition. One man is dressed in a false beard and carrying a bag with "BOMBSKI" painted on it. This is all part of a satire linked to the comments on the card around his neck on which is written: "Bolsheviki moneylender Letitoffnowski" (presumably referring to the bomb). This was the time when scandals were rife about Russian spies funding labour political organisations in Britain and also the publication of the notorious 'Zinoviev Letter' by the Daily Mail in 1924. Apparently sent by a top Russian political figure to the British Communist Party, the letter offered support for a workers revolution. It is now thought to be a forgery aimed at affecting the fortunes of the Labour party in the General Election held a few days after publication.

The Foleshill and Labour Institute was based at 253 Cross Road, the east side of two semi-detached houses next to Edgwick Park School. It had been established after the War and was the home of the Trade Hall Club which had been built in a large area of land beyond the back garden, latterly including a bowling green. It was also the home of the National Union of Ex-Servicemen. Like the photograph above, this view was also taken at the back of the house by the side entrance. The houses at the junction of Canal Road and Cross Road can be seen in the background.

Foleshill Trades and Labour Institute, 253 Cross Road c1925 (Anon.)

The postcard on the left was distributed by supporters of Walter Brandish senior who was standing for the Liberal Party in the Foleshill ward of the Municipal elections of Monday 2nd November 1925. Later to become Lord Mayor of Coventry he owned a motorcycle dealership at 625 Foleshill Road, later to flourish as a large garage elsewhere in Coventry. His son was a famous rider for the Triumph motorcycle team and had a corner of the Isle of Man TT course named after him.

This charming photograph evokes the sort of rural charm still to be found in many parts of Foleshill before the Great War. It was run by the Ely family at the time, only recently returned from America. Abraham, a Coventry weaver, had set out in the late 1880s to escape a declining trade and settled there. He returned in 1899 to his Foleshill roots, with his American wife, Alice, shown here, and their four children. The farm is described on contemporary maps as Edgwick Cottage, which today would be in the middle of the Godiva Trading Estate, north of Cross Road. Until the early twentieth century Cross Road had not been built and the track to the farmhouse began where the junction of Cross Road and Foleshill Road is today. By 1905 Cross Road had been laid out but only a handful of houses had been erected. It was still surrounded by fields. Tragedy had struck the Ely family in 1909 when Abraham was taken ill and died. Alice ran the farm for a few more years before moving into a house in Cross Road that she had built. In the 1920s Alfred Herbert's expanded their factory, first established in 1899. It eventually took up all the land north of Cross Road between Canal Road and Stoney Stanton Road and the farm and its fields were just a memory.

Edgwick Poultry Farm, c1905 (Anon.)

Three Horseshoes, 1007 Foleshill Road, Little Heath 1906 (E.R.) (Warwick Record Office PH350/525)

This cluster of buildings faces north and showing the final stretch of Foleshill Road before becoming Longford Road where it passes the New Inn Bridge. The first few cottages on the left-hand side date from the early nineteenth century. They have a similar style to other cottages along Foleshill Road, dating from this time, that also incorporates a public house, though unlike the Prince William Henry no enlarged early weavers' windows can be seen. Instead, the landlord in the 1860s doubled up as a blacksmith and the original smithy can be seen by where the two men are standing. In the early twentieth century it was a lesser alcoholic outlet known as a beer house rather than a full-blown pub. It was run by Thomas Walling, an ex-tram conductor from Longford. A recently built terrace with neat boundary wall and ironwork in the middle of the picture, beyond the old terrace, is another sign of the expansion of the city. Some of the houses are still there today just before the junction with King George's Avenue which was laid out at the start of the First World War, but the original pub and the older cottages have gone.

A Adderley, Lythalls Lane Supply Stores, Lythalls Lane c1912 (The Stoke Portrait Co)

The 'A' could stand for Alice (41) who was described as a shopkeeper in 1911, and both individuals shown outside are female, or maybe her husband Alfred (40), who was noted as a tinsmith at the time. The houses are still standing but have now been converted back to residences as 70 and 72 Lythalls Lane. Their shop was at the end of a short terrace of four houses, fronting a much older row of houses, Alexandra Terrace. That, like of a number of earlier nineteenth century Foleshill developments, was just a single line of houses built at right angles to the main road.

Foleshill Hall, Lythalls Lane 1917 (Anon.)

This is an important house in Foleshill's history, the impressive frontage dating from the early eighteenth century, but an older manorial building had stood here beforehand. The lane was apparently named after Edward Lythall a tenant of the Hall in the 1830s. It was the centre of a farming estate opposite where Bartlett Close is today, by the bridge over the Coventry to Nuneaton railway. Its proximity to the railway could not have helped its previous rural charm and the wealthy Riley family, whose home it was, eventually sold up in 1914. It was bought by Coventry brewers Phillips and Marriott and was granted a licence in March 1915 with the condition that the land surrounding it should be kept as part of the premises. After conversion, the first publican was Henry Sutton who ran the Horse and Jockey in Hawkesbury Lane that closed in 1916 (see page75). His new wife Edith sent this postcard of their latest pub on their second Christmas as tenants. The pub was demolished in 1989.

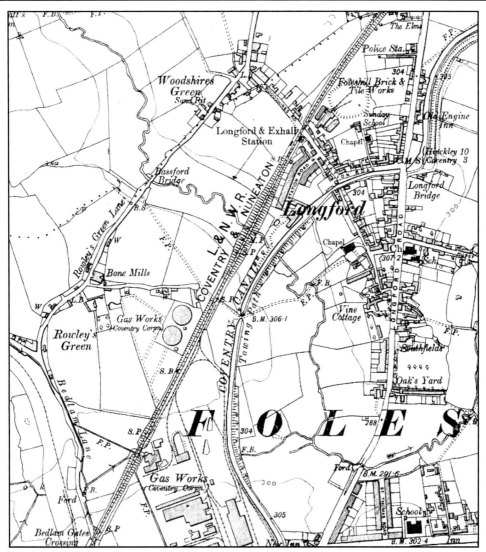

1912 Ordnance Survey Six Inch Map

Despite being firmly within the parish of Foleshill over the centuries Longford became an important population centre in itself. Creating a turnpike trust for the main road and the enclosure of the parish in the eighteenth century helped Longford's growth from what was already a distinctive village into a larger settlement.

The mining industry had spread over the north of Foleshill parish since becoming established during the sixteenth century, involving a large part of the local male population. The weaving industry was also an important form of employment, although it was less conspicuous than in the southern part of the parish as there were fewer of the larger weavers' top-shops and cottage factories. Many weavers would have been operating the smaller, single hand-looms that could be worked in any room of an ordinary cottage.

During the later centuries, a number of new industries developed in Longford even though the Coventry to Nuneaton railway, opened in 1850, offered no goods yard, only a small station. Whilst these new industries were a valuable source of employment they did not contribute to a pleasant environment. The Coventry Fat and Bone Company was a particular offender and later the Coventry Gas Works, as essential as it was, would not have made a good neighbour. Neither would the Foleshill Brick and Tile Works have enhanced the landscape. Yet probe more carefully around present-day Longford and there is a surprising amount that survives of the more attractive side of the village. This is especially so alongside the canal and in some of the backstreets and even elements along the man road. This is despite a number of original buildings that have not survived. But it is still possible to get a feel of early industrial Foleshill here, more so than in districts further south. It is still possible to understand the conclusion of Whites Directory of 1874 in describing Longford as *'a pleasant well-built village chiefly inhabited by ribbon weavers'*.

Windmill Road (formerly Windmill Lane) c1925 (Teesee)

Until the first decade of the twentieth century, Windmill Lane was unpopulated at the Longford Road end in contrast to the nineteenth century collection of cottages at the section towards Hall Green. All development would have been post-1775 as the lane was a creation of the Enclosure Act. According to the 1775 enclosure map, the windmill that gave its name to the road would have been located on its north side near where Recreation Road was built. This view is taken from the junction of Windmill Road and Longford Road showing the build-up of housing that took place before the First World War. Terraced housing was set out on the north side of Windmill Lane linking up with a stretch on the east side of Longford Road with St Thomas Road opposite the trees above forming the third side of the triangle. The trees on the right are what is left of the old country lane. The land behind them had been laid out as a cemetery a few years before the First World War. The large house peeping through the vegetation was its lodge. Dovedale Road took up the land in the foreground when it was laid out in 1930.

Dovedale Cinema, Dovedale Avenue 1929 (Appleby)

This unusually shaped triangular frontage was forced on this cinema by the angled intersection of Windmill Road with Dovedale Avenue. When it opened in 1929 it could seat an audience of more than a 1000, reflecting the recent growth of this area of Foleshill. Like most Coventry cinemas it has gone through many different identities including the Rivoli and the Ritz, losing much of its charming period details in the process. After a spell in the 1970s as an Asian cinema, it was eventually closed. Today it is closed with much of its architectural details, so well-illustrated here, either destroyed or concealed. The houses in Dovedale Avenue were erected soon after the cinema been built.

Coventry Road, Longford c1913 (Waterman)

In both views the Longford landmark of St Thomas's Church is prominent. The road on the left by the tram post is Lady Lane with the charming old building that was once the post office, alongside. Lady Lane is worth a chapter in itself, with a fascinating collection of buildings. Although most were condemned as unfit for habitation and demolished in 1970, enough remains to show what it would have been like to live here in the mid-nineteenth century – a hive of industry with all the working weavers. The view below is looking south towards Coventry with the back of the weavers' top-shops, at the start of Hurst Road, showing to the left of St Thomas's Church tower and 'The Yews', a large house, on the immediate left. Both feature in later views. The main road is straight and wide, a legacy of being turnpiked in the eighteenth century.

LONGFORD, near COVENTRY.   SIDWELL, MERIDEN.

Coventry Road, Longford c1905 (Sidwell)

Market Square (Longford Square), Longford c1905 (Sidwell)

Both views on this page give a better insight into the tight-knit community of Longford that the views of the wide Longford Road cutting through the village cannot. All these mid-nineteenth century cottages in Market Square are still standing today but are homes rather than shops. The brickwork has been hidden behind pebble-dashing or paint. Fortunately, the one exception is that with the distinctive chequerboard brickwork. Even the grand Salem Chapel in Lady Lane, partially shown on the far left, is still standing.

Hurst Lane, Longford c1907 (J.P.)

Over the last 110 years, Hurst Lane has gone from a quiet country lane (see the thatched cottage in the distance) to being Hurst Road and becoming a cul-de-sac. It is no longer a rat run between Longford and Alderman's Green, giving it back a little more peace. Most of the buildings in the foreground remain in place. Especially pleasing is the rare survival of four mid-nineteenth century weavers' top-shops on the corner of Longford Road, shown on the left. It is disappointing, if understandable, that their large 'top-shop' windows (just out of shot) serving the weaving looms have been replaced by much smaller, better insulated versions, however, the original design can still be appreciated. St Thomas's Church grounds opposite remain largely unchanged and attractively landscaped.

Station Road (later Sydnall Road), Longford 1907 (E.R.)

It is interesting to compare these two views, taken six years apart, at different times of the year and from slightly different perspectives. The photograph above, taken in winter, captures the off-licence and grocer on the right at 2, Station Road. Just out of the picture on the corner of Station Road and Bedworth Road was a blacksmith's shop which was still operating when this photograph was taken. The view below was taken in spring, with the canal bank utilised as an allotment showing the young vegetables planted in rows. The trees just beyond the entrance to Union Place are now in leaf. The awnings of the Lockhurst Lane Co-op can be seen on the far right, only opened in 1911 and therefore not shown in the view above. It is not difficult to tie all these buildings into the street today, although the normal process of improvement has affected their appearance. Some attractive unaltered facades can be seen around the corner in Bedworth Road.

Station Road (later Sydnall Road), Longford c1913 (Waterman)

Photo by E. H. Johnson.

Widening of Longford Canal Bridge.

Widening Longford Canal Bridge 20 April 1912 (Coventry Graphic)

In order to take the first steam trams between Coventry and Bedworth in 1884, it was clear that all three canal bridges along Foleshill Road would need widening and strengthening. By 1912, further work was needed at Longford because of the lowering of the bridge caused by mining subsidence. It had become so bad that some canal barges had trouble passing under it. The opportunity was taken to further widen the bridge to cope with the increasing traffic.

Station Road West (later Grindle) Road, Longford 1907 (E.R.)

Originally known as Station Road West (and renamed in the 1930s to avoid confusion with the similarly named road in Great Heath), Grindle Road had just been completed when this photograph was taken, hence the state of the road. Apart from the gas lamp and the iron railings this street has retained much of its original uniformity today. The good quality brick and contrasting stone lintels remain unadorned, making an attractive street scene. However, the view is difficult to reproduce today due to the ranks of parked cars.

Bedworth Road 1907 (E.R.)

This view shows the continuation of Longford Road, where it becomes the Bedworth Road, north of the Longford canal bridge. Older cottages on the immediate right are mixed with the new, such as the semi-detached houses on the left and the terraced houses on the right, further up the road. The tracks of the Coventry to Bedworth tramway, opened in 1900, can be seen in the centre of the road, so quick and easy transport to work in Coventry or Bedworth would no longer be a problem for anyone who moved here. Only a few older cottages remain today beyond this point. The couple on the right and the shop beyond have been demolished to make way for the car park of the Longford Engine pub. Even the houses on the left, new in 1907, were later demolished to make way for Oban Road.

The Yews, Longford c1905 (Sidwell)

The Yews, 198 Longford Road, can be seen to the left of the south facing view of Longford Road on page 57. At the time, it was the home of the generously named Herbert Charles Pickard Masser who had been born and raised in Longford, and then became the local doctor for many years until his death in 1915. The Massers were a prominent family in Longford who lived in one of the grandest houses in the village called Southfields. The Oakmoor estate has been built on its site, next door to the medical centre. Herbert was born at Southfields in 1842 and was involved in local politics and church activities all his life. The Massers also offered significant support in the construction of St Thomas' Church; the foundation stone was laid in 1873. In 1916 an impressive reredos screen was donated in memory of Charles. The Yews is still standing behind a tall fence with its brickwork now rendered.

Longford Brigade Hospital (Naval) c1916-17 (Johnson)

Longford Naval Hospital was one of a number of private hospitals/convalescent homes, set up in the First World War by local philanthropists to look after wounded soldiers. Most were official Voluntary Aided Detachment (VAD) establishments run by the Red Cross, but unusually the Longford Hospital was under the auspices of St John's Ambulance. It was also the only one in Coventry that specialised in naval personnel.

The hospital was based in the home of Longford's vicar, Rev. William Dore Rudgard in Hurst Lane, known as The Grange. It had been built in the late 1880s behind the church and was a substantial residence of twelve rooms, so for a man without a family there was plenty of space. Dore had worked in the parish since 1885, originally as a curate and from 1904 as vicar. As, perhaps, can be gathered from his photograph, Rudgard seemed to be a person who held himself in quite a high regard, assuming the position of Commandant together with a uniform that fitted the role! He did work hard raising funds and organising various amusements and outings for the sailors. Over the course of the War 135 patients passed through his house. It is possible that the dog was part of the therapy.

The vicar had many official appointments; the Workhouse Committee, the Foleshill Military Tribunal as well as being elected Warwickshire County Councillor.

When the Reverend Rudgard died in 1926 he was still vicar of Longford, having worked in the parish for 41 years and also Rural Dean of Monks Kirby and chaplain of the Order of St John of Jerusalem. He left a fortune of more than £25,000 to his secretary, gardener and housekeeper.

It affords us the greatest pleasure this week to reproduce a picture of the Rev. W. Dore Rudgard, M.A., Rector of Longford, who is undoubtedly one of the most industrious men clerical or lay, in Warwickshire. He is commandant of Longford Brigade Hospital (Naval), and the voluntary work he is accomplishing in the tribunal courts and other military circles is most invaluable to the country.

The Rector of Longford 29 September 1916 (Coventry Graphic)

Hugh Gaitskell with the Lord Mayor, W H Malcolm at the Gasworks 1948 (Anon.)

These photographs are taken from an album that was specially put together to celebrate the year that Cllr Malcolm was Lord Mayor of Coventry, shown here in both photographs wearing his mayor chain. This was an especially noteworthy occasion as Hugh Gaitskell, later to be the leader of the Labour Party, was visiting Coventry in his role as Minister of Fuel and Power (shown carrying a folder in both photographs). He had been appointed after the dreadful winter of 1947 when coal supplies were running short and essential services that relied on this fuel such as gas and electricity were under threat. The visit to Coventry was more a flag-waving exercise than offering any real insights.

The original gasworks (opened in 1909) did not have as much visual impact on Longford as it might have as it was hidden on the far side of the railway and canal that flanked Longford's west side. The German designed gas holder was built in 1929/30 as part of an extension to the works. The gasholder was demolished in 2002 to make way for the Arena stadium and retail park.

Ministry party with gas holder behind 1948 (Anon.)

A Local "Improvement."

The rapid expansion of the city and its encroachment on the rural surroundings frequently creates convenience at the expense of the picturesque, as may be seen from the above photos which show Bedlam Lane, Foleshill, before and after the recent widening.

The "improvement" may be appreciated by those who desire wide roads for traffic purposes, but the wholesale obliteration of hedge-rows and other rural features cannot fail to evoke a sentimental sigh from those who knew this haunt years ago. The work involved the demolition of the cottage which is seen embowered by trees in the photo on the right, and a very commercial looking road now stretches over the site.

The development and widening of the road has been necessitated by its favourable position near the new L. and N.W. loop line and the Corporation Gas Works.

Bedlam Lane Improvement, Longford 27 February 1914 (Coventry Graphic)

Understandable regret at the changes that were being brought to even the most rural parts of Foleshill parish was being expressed in this article on the changes to Bedlam Lane. Such changes were minor compared to the fate of this part of Bedlam Lane today that has been covered by Phoenix Way near the entrance to Arena Park. The view is looking north just beyond where the, then new, loop railway line crossed the lane.

Woodshires Road, Longford.

Woodshires Road, Woodshires Green c1925 (Teesee)

With the building of the Coventry to Nuneaton railway in the mid-nineteenth century Woodshires Green became somewhat cut off from Longford centre. It helped it to retain its distinct identity that the many hamlets of Foleshill displayed in the nineteenth century, despite the misleading caption given to the postcard. Its separate identity is weaker today as modern housing has swamped the original centre shown here. The nineteenth century cottages on the right still survive as do others in Wilson Lane, near the junction shown here. The houses on the left were the first of the early twentieth century intrusions. Strictly speaking most of this scene is outside the historic Foleshill boundary which cuts across the road by the tree.

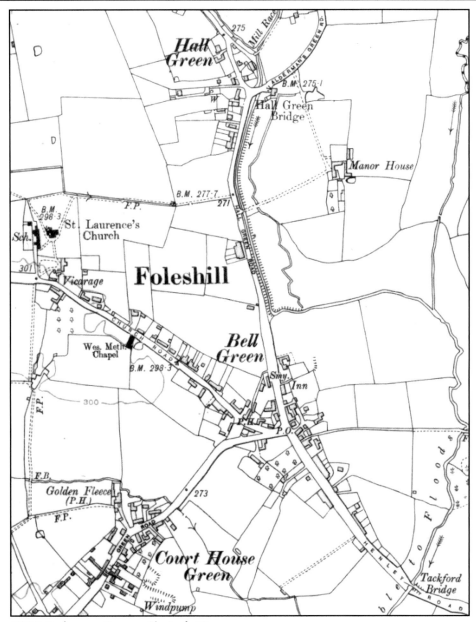

1912 Ordnance Survey Six Inch Map

Throughout Foleshill's earlier history Bell Green was only a hamlet in Foleshill, but for the last few centuries it has overshadowed the ancient centre of the parish around St Laurence Church in Old Church Road (previously Church Lane). In close proximity, there are other historic hamlets of Courthouse Green, Henley Green and Hall Green all of which have given their names to modern suburban districts of Coventry.

At the beginning of the twentieth century, their respective populations fitted into the standard Foleshill pattern consisting of a mix of weavers, coal miners and agricultural workers. Their homes were a miscellaneous collection of cottages strung out along the country roads.

Many of the buildings had their origins as squatters' homes but after the enclosure of the open fields in 1775, their tenure was made official. Although many were originally mud and thatch, by the nineteenth century the majority had been rebuilt and displayed the characteristic chequerboard brickwork so often found in north Warwickshire. Despite the tremendous changes that the twentieth century has brought, amazingly many still survive, yet over the years concrete rendering and modernised doors and windows have made it difficult to appreciate their original appearance. Fortunately, some of the old photographs, shown here, help to give an idea of what the street scene was like when they were first built. Whilst the photographs show there were fewer three-storey weavers' top-shops in these hamlets there is still other architectural evidence for the ribbon weaving industry apart from what the contemporary censuses confirm.

St Laurence's Church, Old Church Road 1904 (Anon.)

The above scene captures the rural setting that was typical of Foleshill for much of its history. It shows the north-west side of the church on the footpath leading to Longford. To the right is the school built partly in the churchyard in 1750 by the vicar. It was one of the first day schools to be established in Coventry (see opposite). The church has undergone many changes in its history and it appears almost nothing is left of the original twelfth-century chapel, although the font dates from this period. The tower is shown below being repaired in 1923 by J. Jones, a local builder. It is the oldest addition dating from the fifteenth century. Over the past four centuries much of the rest of the church has been rebuilt and added to, especially in the last 150 years, as a result of population growth and the idiosyncrasies of different vicars. More recent changes were brought about by an incendiary bomb in 1940 which destroyed the nave roof. Today the church is a rather messy but interesting hotch-potch of these alterations. Despite the regular expansion of the accommodation, at one time seating 900 people, by the nineteenth century Foleshill parish desperately needed additional churches. So in 1841 St Paul's was built in Great Heath, followed in 1874 by St Thomas's at Longford.

St Laurence's Church, Old Church Road 1923 (Winterbourne)

The Vicarage, Old Church Road 1907 (E.R.)

The old vicarage dates back to 1745 and is still to be found today south of the church, now used as a care home. Like the church, it experienced a number of alterations and extensions in the nineteenth century and more recent extensions to the care home have almost tripled its size. The new vicarage is to be found nearby, still within the grounds, but with other parts of the estate sold off for housing, there is little of the original garden left.

Foleshill C of E School, Old Church Road 1928 (The Racine Company)

Foleshill School was the oldest in the area having been founded in 1750 beside St Laurence Church. It was rebuilt and enlarged during the nineteenth and twentieth centuries before a new school was developed in 1965 in the old Vicarage garden. Eventually the old school, seen here, was demolished. Although photographs of school buildings are not very common there are always historic class photographs that crop up. A photographer is commissioned by the school and sales can always be guaranteed. This postcard was taken by the Racine Company and then used as a receipt for the sales and sent to Mr H Hancock, the headmaster from the mid-1920s until the Second World War. It shows that the total bill came to £4-8s-0d. Assuming the postcards cost about 3d each that would mean more than 300 photographs of the different classes would have been produced for sale to the pupils.

Old Church Road 1907 (E.R.)

The Wesleyan Chapel in Old Church Road is the point of reference for both these views, although it appears in neither. The building is largely unchanged since it was built in 1848 to replace the original of 1813 and it is still a place of worship. The view above, facing east, is taken from beside the chapel which is to the right. Amazingly for Foleshill, most of the houses on the left-hand side of this view are still standing, but the hedges have gone to be replaced by fences. There is hardly any original brickwork visible now, as all the houses have been rendered and in the inter-war years Pearson Avenue was built between the first two sets of cottages on the left. Modern houses have also filled the land on the right.

Today, in the view below facing west would also show Dudley Street opposite the house on the right and Pearson Avenue has been built between the near and far sets of cottages in the centre of the picture. Note the exceptionally large window in the side of the cottage in the distance at 80 Old Church Road (see inset). This is a rare view of the sort of weaving space that most poor, single-handed weaving loom operators would have been common all over this area of Foleshill, mainly operated by women.

Old Church Road 1907 (E.R.)

Bell Green Carnival, Hall Green Road, 14 June 1913 (Sylvester)

The band is heading towards Bell Green with the brook on the far side and Grindall's Farm (Manor House Farm) beyond. In the front row, on the left is Fred Ward, the Wesleyan Chapel Sunday School Superintendent. The clarinet player in front of the banner, wearing a boater, is George North the Choirmaster at the Wesleyan Chapel.

This view was taken in the field behind the Wesleyan Chapel in Old Church Road, mentioned on the previous page. All those taking part in the procession are members of the congregation. The back of the large chapel can be seen behind the decorated cart. The wagon has been dressed up as a float ready to join the annual carnival.

Bell Green Carnival, Old Church Road 14 June 1913 (Sylvester)

After assembling behind the Wesleyan Chapel the procession came out onto Old Church Road and paraded around the hamlets to the east. This view shows the procession returning to the Wesleyan Chapel in Old Church Road. The blurred outlines of the chapel railings are in the foreground. The houses hidden behind the decorated carriage are visible between the first and second set of cottages on the top view of the previous page.

Bell Green Carnival, Old Church Road 14 June 1913 (Sylvester)

Old Church Road, Bell Green 1907 (E.R.)

These two views demonstrate how much the face of Bell Green has changed over the last hundred years. Both show the eastern end of Old Church Road, the view above is by the junction with Bell Green Road on the left where the tram lines are just visible. The view below is taken near to where the two girls are standing on the right, above.

Almost none of the buildings shown in the first photograph can be seen in the second as most had been demolished. The Bell Hotel, known for most of its life as the Bell, is a notable exception, even if it is only just peeping out on the right-hand side of the road with a flagpole by its roof. The Bell was known for providing accommodation for entertainers at the Coventry Theatre. There is a press photograph of Morecambe and Wise and Roy Castle, taken in the pub bar, in the early 1960s. By the mid-1960s even this famous pub had closed and was demolished. The entrance to Bellview Way, a small housing development, has taken the place of the pub. At least the houses shown below on the left and those in the distance on the right are still standing today. The first few in the group on the left date from the mid-nineteenth century, although the rest of the group are an early twentieth century terraced development.

The Bell Hotel, Old Church Road c1955 (Landscape)

Hall Green Road, Bell Green 1907 (E.R.)

The contrast between these two views, thirty years apart, is obvious in a number of important ways, demonstrating the rapid expansion of Coventry affecting even these far-flung parts of Foleshill. Unsurprisingly the last eighty years have brought even more changes. The Rose and Crown is still there, albeit in the form of its 1958 re-build, set back from the road on what was the pub's bowling green. Even in these views we can tell the old pub had expanded by the late 1930s, taking over the cottage next door, remodelled with a suitable matching facade. It can also be seen that housing developments before the Second World War had cleared away the hedges, trees and thatched cottages along the left-hand side of the road as far as Hall Green. The right-hand side remained unchanged until the second half of the twentieth century. It is very unlikely that the writer of the postcard above would still choose to describe it as the '***village where I live***' today.

Hall Green Road, Bell Green c1938 (Richards)

Henley Road, Bell Green 1907 (E.R.)

Terraces of recently constructed Edwardian houses can be seen in the distant left and right alongside the older cottages, and scaffolding for more being built can be seen at the end of the terrace on the left. Many of the houses accommodated miners working at the nearby Alexandra Colliery in Wyken, although Daniel Burdett, the last silk spinner, was still working here at this time. In the foreground is Flavell's baker, grocer and off-licence shop in the grandly titled Bell Green House.

Bell Green Wesleyan F C 18 October 1919 (Sylvester)

The Wesleyan Chapel in Old Church Road has already featured in a number of captions and here is further testimony to the central part it played as an informal community centre in Bell Green life. Football teams could be found all over Coventry playing in a variety of different leagues including the 'Old Boys League' in which the Bell Green team played. There did not seem to be an obvious criterion for membership as although the league did include representatives from other chapels, they also included a Binley Colliery team and one from O'Brien's cycle factory in Foleshill Road. The Bell Green Wesleyans were having a reasonable year as a note on the back states: "*This photo is of our football team at Chapel. They have only lost about three matches. They are not like the City, lose every one*"!

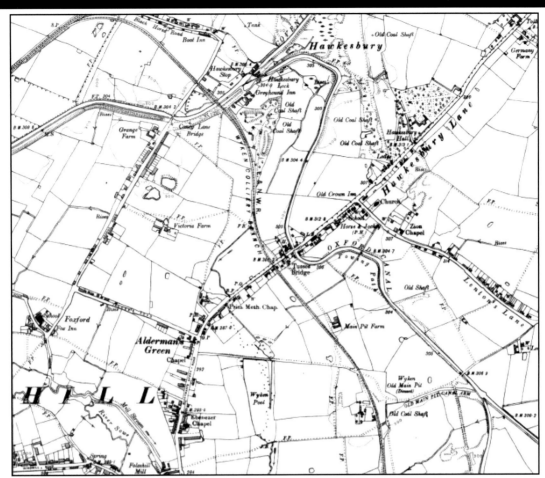

1912 Ordnance Survey Six Inch Map

There is a certain irony in the fact that this corner of Foleshill parish, most isolated from the large centres of population, should have a history of industrial activity dating back several centuries. The presence of coal mining from Tudor times and the construction of an important canal junction in the eighteenth century, several railways in the nineteenth century and a power station in the twentieth century made this less of a rural idyll than it might have been. Strangely the area also contains the only two surviving potential Foleshill manor houses, Tolldish Hall and Hawkesbury Hall. In most other respects this area of Foleshill is unremarkable conforming to most of the norms of development for the parish as a whole. Waste land alongside the roads offered the only opportunity for squatter housing a few centuries ago, especially for those working in the mines. By the time the weaving industry came to the district and especially after the 1775 Foleshill Enclosure Act, land tenure was more settled and more permanent homes were constructed.

Today, this area provides some of the clearest evidence of the original settlements, made up of buildings strung along the old roads and lanes, known as ribbon development. The buildings are mainly made up of cottages from the late eighteenth and nineteenth centuries, together with twentieth century intrusions. They are most noticeable along the roads near to the hamlet centres of Alderman's Green and Hawkesbury. One complicating factor in this north-eastern part of the parish is its eccentric boundary that seems to cut through what are otherwise homogeneous communities. For example, most of the eastern side of Hawkesbury Lane is in Walsgrave on Sowe parish. Individuals' attitudes as to what makes a coherent community develop to reflect relationships that are more important than respecting traditional territorial boundaries, so for the purposes of this book the whole of Hawkesbury Lane (also known as Tusses Bridge in part) as well as Lenton's Lane will be included here. It should also be noted that the modern Coventry boundary cuts through this area just north of Lenton's Lane. It would be much simpler if this area would have retained its old collective name of Tackley.

Alderman's Green Road, Alderman's Green 1926 (Teesee)

The pebble-dashed houses on the right are still standing as a tribute to the initiative of the early twentieth century Co-op movement in Coventry. This area originally had its own organisation known as the Alderman's Green Hope Industrial Co-operative Society which had been absorbed by the Stoney Stanton Road Prudential Co-operative Society and then in 1905 by the Coventry Perseverance Co-operative Society. The local society had already built several cottages together with their shop (around the corner on the right) by the end of the nineteenth century, but the former had been condemned as unsanitary by the Foleshill District Council as it had inadequate drainage. The Coventry Co-op concluded that any money spent on these houses would be wasted, so in 1910 they agreed to build five houses in their place, shown here on the right. They also agreed to build a street with more houses if there was a demand and so Co-operative Street was constructed beside the end house on the right, before the First World War. In an area of rather undistinguished architecture, these houses stand out for their distinctive style.

Methodist Church & Memorial, Alderman's Green 1926 (Teesee)

Much of the Foleshill area, including Longford, Bell Green, Hawkesbury and Alderman's Green were centres of non-conformist worship during the industrial development of the nineteenth century. The evidence can be found in the number of chapels that each of these areas was able to support. Despite appearances, there is only one chapel in this view, although there were two others in Alderman's Green Road as well as another one nearby in Lentons Lane, all built in the mid-nineteenth century and all Methodist in denomination. The Ebenezer Free Methodist chapel on the left was built in 1898 and a Jubilee Hall on the far right added in 1908, with a Men's Institute behind (and out of sight) in 1921. In the centre is the Methodist Sunday School built around 1850. In the foreground is the War Memorial to the fallen of Alderman's Green in the First World War unveiled by Mayor W H Grant in November 1920.

Alderman's Green Road 1907 (E.R.)

This sequence of the following three photographs offers as complete a view of what a typical nineteenth century community in north Foleshill would have looked like as anywhere in this book. The twentieth century developments affecting the majority of the parish to the south had not quite reached here yet. Only the occasional Edwardian intrusion can be seen, such as the semi-detached houses on the immediate left above and the detached house in the centre-left below. Confirmation of this belief comes from an article in the Coventry Standard of 14 July 1916 where the writer reflected on a recent visit to the area and concluded *'the modern rush has left this spot almost untouched'*. All these views were taken on the same day in 1907 by Ernest Ratledge from Rugby who photographed all the streets of Coventry and district in that year. He then made postcards from the glass plates, but they were only produced in small numbers and therefore their survival is rare but invaluable. By including children Ratledge would hope to encourage sales to their parents. The view above is looking northwards with The Bird in Hand just behind the children. The couple of cottages beyond have local listing today being late eighteenth century in date. The house on the right has a rare example of a large side window on the ground floor, typical of a simple silk weaver's single hand loom operation, like that in the cottage on page 66. In the view below Ratledge has moved a few yards up the road towards Hawkesbury, the first and third buildings on the left are sets of terraced cottages at right angles to the road with the Wesleyan Methodist Chapel, dating from 1840, just before the row of cottages (shown in more detail on the next page). The second building on the left is the only building still surviving from this view.

Alderman's Green Road 1907 (E.R.)

Alderman's Green Road 1907 (E.R.)

Ratledge has again moved further northwards along the road from the previous view and the terrace of older cottages is now prominent. On the left is a distinctive tree near the entrance to Jacker's Road also visible in the previous views. The couple of sets of cottages just beyond Jacker's Road are all that is left of this collection of buildings today. The old Miners Arms (the large building in the distance seen to the left of the group of children) was replaced by a modern building in 1968 and that also was demolished around 2010. Today most of the buildings fronting the road have been built in the last fifty years and it has begun to resemble more a featureless suburb than the community of old. The buildings that have survived need to be cherished although they too have their historic features hidden behind modern rendering and replacement doors and windows.

The Elephant & Castle, Tusses Bridge, Alderman's Green Lane 1926 (Teesee)

Tusses Bridge over the canal has given its name to a small district in itself rather than just the boundary between Alderman's Green and Hawkesbury. The Elephant and Castle pub only recently closed in 2011 although the cottage beside it had long gone. For the visitor today the greatest change has come with the raising and widening of the road to level the hump-backed bridge, seen here, over the Oxford Canal. The solution has created a sort of fly-over which has hidden the pub from view, apart from its roof. Today any sense of rural charm that might have been retained is rather spoilt by the M6 passing over the road behind where the photographer stood.

The Dock, Oxford Canal, Tusses Bridge, Alderman's Green Lane 1926 (Teesee)

Tusses Bridge was a useful stop on the Oxford Canal before its junction with the Coventry Canal at Sutton Stop. A set of moorings on the west side of Tusses Bridge would encourage boats to stop and shop for supplies from the local shops as well as have a beer in the Elephant and Castle. The boatyard on the right was a valued facility. A canal barge is being repaired undercover in one shed and another has its hull upside down in the open. The notice on the boat in the foreground tells us that it belongs to James Hambridge, registered in Coventry; it also displays some characteristic narrow boat decoration.

Tusses Bridge (Hawkesbury Lane) 1907 (E.R.)

The road is Hawkesbury Lane but this area is known as Tusses Bridge coming just after the canal bridge. Much has changed in this scene today with all the cottages to the right having been demolished except the terraced block in the centre of the picture, although it too may be under threat given that it has been partially boarded up for some time. It would be a shame to lose this last remnant of old Hawkesbury especially as it has its original slate tiles and has escaped being rendered. As a result, it is still showing its distinctive chequerboard brickwork like the cottage on the right.The Horse and Jockey pub is the first building beyond the terraced block and would be an important part of any community, but it had closed in 1916 and the licence taken over by the Foleshill Old Hall.

Hawkesbury Lock, Sutton Stop 1926 (Teesee)

The main canal that snakes through the Foleshill area is the Coventry Canal, started in 1769 and eventually was extended for 38 miles to Fradley, north of Lichfield. The Oxford Canal was completed later and they later joined at the Hawkesbury Junction otherwise known today as Sutton Stop. This lock is at the point where the two meet, looking back towards the Oxford Canal. The buildings mainly date from the first half of the nineteenth century and remarkably few have been lost. Amongst those that have been demolished are the cottages on the left of the view above, but fortunately much else shown is better looked after today. This is due, the site, split between Coventry City Council and Nuneaton and Bedworth Borough Council, being jointly recognised as a Conservation Area since 1976. One of the protected buildings is 32 Sutton Stop seen through the iron bridge in the view below. Until 1850 it was used to store gunpowder and then, until 1930, for fitting out boats, as it was at the time shown here. The canopy conceals the winches for hauling cargo from the boats to first-floor level and the double doors for storage on the ground floor. Since 1930 it has only been used for residential purposes. The impressive bridge crosses the point where the Oxford Canal meets the Coventry Canal alongside 32 Sutton Stop. Clearly, cast on the side is the date it was made, 1837, and the factory, Britannia Foundry, Derby.

The Iron Bridge, Sutton Stop 1926 (Teesee)

W H Topp, Hawkesbury Lane c1910 (J.P.)

The trap carries the name W H Topp, a baker whose shop was amongst the group of houses in Hawkesbury Lane shown on the right of the photograph on the previous page. Next door to William was Samuel Topp, his father, who was a grocer at the time but had also trained as a baker in Alderman's Green in the 1860s. The view of the horse and trap is outside the distinctive iron and slate Hawkesbury Iron Church.

When the church was built it was in Walsgrave on Sowe parish. It was established in 1860 to serve the mining community in the area. As in many other parts of Coventry, the Church of England was rather late in having a presence in this community and consequently their spiritual needs had been served for many years by the various non-conformist chapels in Hawkesbury and nearby Alderman's Green. What the church did bring to Hawkesbury was education. Until a separate school was built two years later, part of the church functioned as a day school for the area. In 1908 part of Hawkesbury came under Longford parish and responsibility for the church was taken over by St Thomas's. The Iron Church was now known as St Matthew's Mission. As the original name suggests the building was built of corrugated iron with a cast-iron framework and a slate roof. The small bell tower was a notable feature. Although the walls of the church were later covered with render the building remained difficult to maintain and it was closed in 1963. The church was demolished and today its site, between the Crown pub and Tynemouth Close, is occupied by a housing estate.

Iron Church Hawkesbury c1910 (J.P.)

Hawkesbury School House 1920 (Anon.)

When Hawkesbury School moved from the church in 1862 it was to a new building on the opposite side of Lenton's Lane overlooking its old home. Part of the school can be seen behind the tree on the right of this photograph. The schoolhouse, home of the headmaster, was built to the west of the school. The school was closed in 1968 and subsequently both buildings were demolished and housing erected on the site.

Baptist Chapel, Lenton's Lane, Hawkesbury 1907 (E.R.)

Whilst the chapel is still standing in Lenton's, Lane its façade is somewhat changed from that shown here. The front has gained a porch, the windows have been squared off, the pediment is no longer triangular and brickwork is hidden under white paint. Old inscriptions indicate most of these changes occurred in 1921. It seems they may have reused the distinctive windows shown here on a side extension. Originally it was known as the Zion Baptist Chapel, built in 1845 to seat 186 worshipers. Baptists from Cow lane Chapel in Coventry had been preaching in this area since 1816 and established a base in Thomas Harrison's house on the eastern side of Hawkesbury Lane. Interestingly baptisms were sometimes performed in the nearby Oxford Canal, across the road in front of the chapel. The building was also known as Wyken Square Baptist Chapel. The term was applied to the short stretch of Lenton's Lane up to Hawkesbury Lane. It seems a singularly inappropriate name for somewhere that was not a square and not in Wyken.

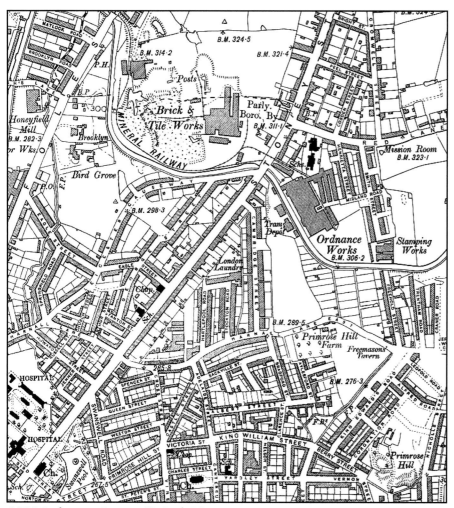

1904 Ordnance Survey Six Inch Map

Both Stoney Stanton Road and Foleshill Road share a similar status in that they are used as shorthand for districts of Coventry, and both are located mainly in the historic parish of Foleshill except for their southernmost sections. For completeness, all of Stoney Stanton Road, like Foleshill Road is included in this book. This section deals mainly with the southern half of the road, outside the parish of Foleshill, which only starts at Red Lane.

The route has medieval origins as a track leading to Leicester across the heathlands north of Coventry, via Leicester Causeway. The current road layout dates from when it was turnpiked in 1831.The stretch from St Mark's Church to the canal was a completely new road across open fields, hence it is especially straight and wide in this section. Before, the old road started where Leicester Causeway branched off Harnall Lane and then joined the original section of the road at Priestley's Bridge. This older section of the road up to Paradise was known various names including Red House Lane or Causeway Lane. The new southern section was labelled on the 1851 Board of Health map as Leicester New Road. The impact of the new section of road from the Coventry and Warwickshire Hospital up to Priestley's Bridge on the subsequent development was rather different to the lower Foleshill Road, in that housing estates were developed behind the road as early as the mid-nineteenth century. The narrow ribbon development characteristic of early Foleshill Road housing was found along the older northern section of Stoney Stanton Road.

The arbitrary northern limit for what is being described as 'lower' Stoney Stanton Road is the junction with Bright Street. Bright Street is the furthest part of one of the three Freehold Land Society housing estates that covered much of this part of Stoney Stanton Road from the 1850s until their demolition in the late twentieth century. These estates were the result of a working-class housing movement that started in Birmingham in the late 1840s and spread to Coventry soon after. The Coventry Freehold Land Society's two estates (the Lant and the Smith) stretched along the west side of the road from the hospital to just beyond Stanton Street. The Coventry & Warwickshire Artizans Freehold Land Society Red Lane estate covered the corner of Red Lane and Stoney Stanton Road up to Cromwell Street in the former and Bright Street in the latter. The object of these organisations was to buy up an area of land then lay out the roads, drains and paths and sell off building plots to their working-class members at a cheaper price than would otherwise be possible. They had an important role in shaping the development in this part of Coventry. Today only a handful of houses in Russell Street are left of the Lant and Smith estates.

Stoney Stanton Road 1907 (E.R.)

Above can be seen the start of Stoney Stanton Road, stretching into the distance by its junction with Bird Street on the right. St Mark's Church is the sole survivor of this view today, although the building being built on the left still stands, shown below. St Mark's was closed for worship in 1972 and has been used by a number of organisations, such as a health centre and a base for a local radio station. It has recently become a centre of Christian worship again. On the opposite side of the road, with the bay window is the Hospital Inn, named after the Coventry and Warwickshire Hospital that opened in the extensive grounds beyond in 1867, two years before St Mark's was consecrated. The pub closed in 1918 when it was taken over as part of the expansion of the hospital site which explains the building work in the picture where a home for the nurses is being erected. The foundation stone had been laid by the Countess of Craven in 1906. The view below is taken a little further up Stoney Stanton Road a few years later and shows the now completed building from the opposite direction. Plans have been made to convert the surviving building into student accommodation and save its facade. The original 1867 hospital can be seen on its right.

Coventry & Warwickshire Hospital c1909 (Kingsway)

Coventry & Warwickshire Hospital. Out-Patient Department c1910 (Appleby)

Coventry's economic resurgence in the late nineteenth and early twentieth century had seen its population boom and the hospital struggled to cater to its needs. A number of new buildings were planned, the first of which was the nurses' home. The new octagonal outpatient department, above, was opened in 1909. In-patients care had almost tripled since 1890 but outpatient cases more than quadrupled. To judge from the numbers of those in the outpatient department the experience was at least as long as today, although the environment has improved considerably. Some of the new wards, as shown below, incorporated balconies that allowed beds to be wheeled outside (at all times of the year!), to enjoy the perceived health benefits of a fresh air cure that was considered the universal panacea for illness in Edwardian times. The octagonal building described above has been saved as part of a scheme to provide student accommodation.

Coventry & Warwickshire Hospital. Balconies on New Wing c1910 (Appleby)

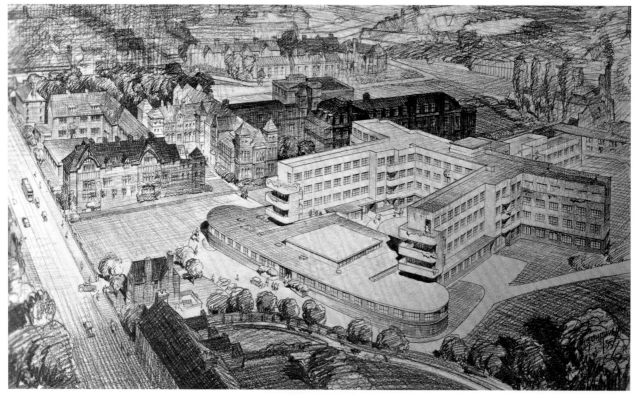

Coventry & Warwickshire Hospital Proposed Building c1936 (Anon.)

Coventry's population had continued to boom in the interwar years and the Coventry and Warwickshire Hospital needed to expand again. The layout of the hospital described in previous pages can be gauged from the architect's sketch produced for the 1930s hospital extensions. Stoney Stanton Road is in the foreground with the 1910 extension to left. The 1867 hospital is in the centre and the Art Deco design for the new building in the foreground. Although most of the work was completed just before the War, subsequent bombing destroyed much of the building. The amount of damage can be judged from the later aerial view below, where Stoney Stanton Road is at the top of the picture. Nothing has survived of the 1867 hospital, however, the 1930 development, viewed here from the rear, was able to be patched up and, with temporary buildings, continued to be the main centre for medical care until the gradual transfer to the new Walsgrave Hospital complex from 1966. Now, most of the city centre site that has served Coventry's medical needs for more than 150 years is being redeveloped. Fortunately, some of the Edwardian buildings alongside Stoney Stanton Road have been retained for alternatives uses.

Coventry & Warwickshire Hospital aerial view c1960 (Aerofilms)

Stoney Stanton Road c1908 (Anon.)

The first residential buildings beyond the hospital complex as far as Howard Street were nearly all three storeys high. Built in the 1850s, before the hospital, the large terraces reflected the status of the location, near the city centre but away from its insalubrious living conditions and being on a tram route just added to the convenience Apart from the neighbouring Hillfields district, these were some of the first residential building estates outside the city centre.. The Alma Inn on the far corner of Howard Street, above right, is also shown below left with its distinctive dormer windows. The name reflects the time at which it was built, commemorating the first battle of the Crimean War. The mainly residential west side of the road up to this point, perhaps reflecting its design as one of the Coventry Freehold Land Society's estates, was not echoed on the east side being more frequently interspersed with shops. The start of Hayfield Terrace on the right, below, hosts a butcher and a pawnbroker before reverting to three-storey residential buildings.

Stoney Stanton Road 1907 (E.R.)

Rose & Woodbine, 78, Stoney Stanton Road c1904 (Anon.)

The Rose and Woodbine shows the date 1898 above its name, carved in stone. Although this was the date the pub was rebuilt it had already been on this site for fifty years from when the area was first developed. Its location on the corner of Harnall Lane West and Stoney Stanton Road guaranteed a good passing trade. Whilst the building still survives its future is in doubt having been closed since 2010 and the settled community which it once served has shrunk due to later developments. One of the earliest landlords in the new building was F J Hibbell, who we can assume stands in the entrance with his wife. He only stayed for a few years from 1903 to 1905.

Public houses played an important part in the community of all areas of the city. Some were purpose-built, like the Alma Inn featured on the previous page and the Rose and Woodbine above. It is possible that the Gloucester Arms fits into another category of conversions from residential buildings, as indeed might the Hospital Inn at the start of Stoney Stanton Road. These last two pubs came into being around 1860 which coincided with the collapse of the City's ribbon weaving industry. The market for new houses vanished and the building industry went into a depression that lasted for at least another decade. Conversion of unsalable houses offered a commercial opportunity. The first licensee of the Gloucester Arms, William Chandler received his licence in August 1860, fifty years later George Kaye stands proudly in the doorway as the latest licensee who remained in charge for almost two decades. Unfortunately, the pub, located just south of Harnall Lane East, was closed in 1968 and the site is now part of the new City College Coventry site. Both these views were sold as postcards by the respective landlords as adverts for their trade.

Gloucester Arms, 57, Stoney Stanton Road c1910 (Iliffe)

Stoney Stanton Road 1905 (Anon.)

The pinnacle at the apex of the frontage of the Rose and Woodbine can be made out clearly on the left of the view above and, less clearly, to the right of that below, which tells us that Harnall Lane crosses at this point. Although this is a busy street scene traffic speed is a lot slower so the photographer's elaborate preparation of the wooden glass-plate camera and tripod would not be too much of a problem and the clattering of an oncoming tram would give ample warning of its approach. Below shows the road from the opposite direction a short distance further on. All these buildings on the east side of the road from Harnall Lane East northwards were built at least two decades after those below the junction and were mainly two-storey residential housing. By then the Coventry economy was recovering from the collapse of the ribbon weaving trade. Occasional clues to the existence of this once important industry can be seen such as the large windows at the back of the three-storey building on the right, at the junction of Stanton Street. This was amongst the last of the top-shops to be built, ready to house the latest advanced Jacquard weaving looms. The woman on the immediate left is standing outside the post office at 125 Stoney Stanton Road.

Stoney Stanton Road 1905 (Anon.)

Howard Street, Lant Estate 1907 (E.R.)

These two streets are examples from the two estates that were developed on land bought by the Coventry Freehold Land Society in 1851. The estate names refer to the previous owners of the land mentioned in the 1841 Foleshill Tithe map; the Lant Estate (including Howard, Byron, Jenner and Russell Streets) and the Smith Estate (including Stanton, George and Arthur Streets). Over the next few years the Society laid out the roads and installed drainage and water supplies and then divided up the land into plots which were bought by its members for building a home. Many of the members of the Society were involved in the ribbon trade and some built their houses with a third storey to contain their looms. These can be seen on the far left of Howard Street and to the right of Stanton Street. Unusually, in the case of the later buildings, the large windows necessary for the delicate work was not visible at the front; see the previous page for the rear view of Stanton Street. As in the contemporary estates in Earlsdon and Upper Stoke, the style of the porches are characteristic of the mid-nineteenth century. There is a clear contrast here with the blander but more widespread designs of the Edwardian terraced housing. Although Howard Street still exists today none of the houses that make up this scene survive. Russell Street is in the foreground on the right, marked by Bicknell's greengrocer's shop on the corner. On the right, just before the junction with Jenner Street, is the distinctive globe of the gas light outside the Gate Inn. In the distance are the buildings in Stoney Stanton Road.

Stanton Street, Smith Estate 1907 (E.R.)

__M J Randells (late M J Griffin) Family Butcher, 65 Stoney Stanton Road 1907 (Anon.)__

This close-up of the shop on the corner of Harnall Lane East and Stoney Stanton Road gives an indication of how many people would have been employed by such a business, useful if it is a postcard promoting your enterprise. Unusually the proprietor is a woman, as was the previous owner. It was in 1907 that Mary Randells took over the butchers from Mary J Griffin, whose name is still prominent. Mary is probably one of the two women in the doorway. It is from this point along Stoney Stanton Road that the style of buildings moves from mid to late nineteenth century to reflect the renewed development in the area.

__Stoney Stanton Road c1905 (Anon.)__

We are fortunate to have another in this series of postcards of Stoney Stanton Road as contemporary photographs of it are unusually rare, especially when compared to Foleshill Road. Here can be seen the view to the south with the tower of the Wesleyan Chapel at the corner of Eagle Street on the right. This impressive red brick building was opened in 1898 and held 700 worshippers as well as containing four Sunday school classrooms. The chapel closed in the 1980s and moved to the corner of Howard Street. The original chapel now operates an Islamic centre after being disused for a number of years. By the mid-1880s all the houses and shops on the left had been built. The right side was less well developed after Stanton Road. The third shop on the left is one of the sixteen pawn shops in Coventry at the time, Herbert Evans at number 213; note the pawnbroker sign comprising of three spheres.

Stoney Stanton Road c1905 (Anon.)

Although taken from different directions both photographs show the northern end of lower Stony Stanton Road. They also show the tram cars that plied the route from Broadgate to Bell Green, first opened in 1899. Tram 30, shown below, was one of 12 bought from Wigan four years later. One of Coventry's two tram depots was located alongside the canal at Priestley's Bridge, a few doors up on the left of the view above. On the right was the point where in 1831 the new road connected to the old road at the Leicester Causeway junction. On the left is the impressive façade of the Co-op store's grocery and drapery departments at 297 and 299 Stoney Stanton Road. The store has gone and its land together with that of the old tram depot is now occupied by one of Coventry's mosques. At 270/272, on the corner of Leicester Causeway to the right, is Stanton Coffee Tavern. The view below looking north shows Priestley's Bridge in the distance with the rows of Edwardian terraced housing lining the road the whole way, interspersed with shops such as Jesse Holliday's hardware shop at 243 Stoney Stanton Road and Hull and Raven fancy drapers next door. Today the shops are almost as numerous as the houses.

Tram coming down Stoney Stanton Road c1908 (Anon.)

Naval Gun Barrel at Railway Crossing, Stoney Stanton Road, June 1912 (T-H Co)

This is a very evocative view of a regular event before and during the First World War. The railway branch line serving the Ordnance Works passed over the road just north of Priestley's Bridge carrying the giant 13.5-inch naval gun barrels made at the factory. The line ran from the factory to the right, behind the houses in Ordnance Road, across the road and into the extensive grounds of the Webster Brick and Tile Work and then westwards on to the Coventry to Nuneaton line. Viewed through the smoke, on the right, can be seen three groups of silk weaving top-shops, the remnants of Coventry's major industry from half a century earlier. Below, and almost thirty years later, the same view is shown below and although the level crossing is now redundant and disused, little else seems to have changed. The top-shops can be seen more clearly and even more in the distance, beyond the junction with Peel Street. Almost all these houses have gone but a few are still standing but with only the bottom two levels remaining as their top-shop storey has been removed. Despite Stoney Stanton Road being improved when it was turnpiked in 1831, Priestley's Bridge had remained the original narrow, humpbacked passage over the canal, until the end of the nineteenth century. It was not until 1899 that it and Navigation Bridge further north was widened to allow the trams to be able to pass to Bell Green. Officially, Foleshill parish started near the furthest tram, by the Red Lane junction.

Priestley's Bridge Level Crossing, Stoney Stanton Road 1939 (Priestley)

Ordnance Factory, Ordnance Road c1910 (Harvey Barton)

The Ordnance Works dominated the area to the east of Priestley's Bridge, bordered to the south and east by the loop of the Coventry Canal. It surrounded Smith Street and Henrietta Street and reached Red Lane for half its

Ordnance Road 1904 (Anon.)

length. Various business had been established on the site from the late 1890s and by 1902 it had become an ordnance factory, but it wasn't until 1905 when a consortium of shipbuilders created the Coventry Ordnance Works Ltd, that the site was developed further. The building shown above was the original office block and entrance, alongside the canal in the foreground. The building can also be seen in the background of the amateur snapshot of the woman and her dog sitting on the front wall of 2, Ordnance Road. This terrace was built before the 1905 take-over to house the foremen working at the factory, and they still flank the left-hand side of the road today, although the factory has gone. The front gardens all seem to boast a prolific display of greenery although whether it is made up of vegetables or flowers is not clear.

Ordnance Factory, Ordnance Road c1906 (Jackson & Son)

The sheer scale of the Ordnance Works can be appreciated by the size of the extension being built in 1906. Interestingly, given the way its armaments were to be used in less than a decade, the building was designed and erected by a German firm. It was claimed at the time to be the largest in Europe, but the rest of the factory buildings more than equalled it in size. The First World War led to a greater range of products being produced from the famous 15-inch naval gun barrels to small 4.5-inch Howitzer field guns. The naval guns were the largest in the world at the time and were a product of the naval arms race that contributed to the outbreak of war in 1914.

Naval Gun at Railway Bridge, Narrow Lane (Kingfield Road) c1912 (T-H Co)

The left view shows one of the Ordnance railway engines moving backwards towards the Nuneaton line with its cargo of a 13.5 inch, fifty-ton naval gun barrel. By the time it reached this bridge, just north of the Cash's Kingfield factory, it had travelled across Stoney Stanton Road level crossing, through Webster's Brick and Tile Works, under Foleshill Road and between the Courtaulds factory and the canal. The bridge, like the railway, had been dismantled after closure in 1972. This view has been mistaken for the Coventry Loop Line over Stoney Stanton Road by Navigation Bridge, but it would be impossible for trams being able to pass underneath. The photograph was re-captioned 'Off To The Fray' after the War started.

Red Lane 1907 (E.R.)

The Red Lane Estate is the third estate along Stoney Stanton Road that can be attributed to the work of the Freehold Land Society movement. In this case it was the Coventry and Warwickshire Artizans Freehold Land Society, established in 1851. The Society developed an area of land on the north-east corner of the junction of Red Lane and Stoney Stanton Road laying out Cobden, Cromwell, Bright and Peel Streets. They were named by the society after politicians who were in tune with their political beliefs. Altogether, 262 building plots were laid out for sale. Members of the Society could then be allocated a plot on which they could build a house, paying back the Society over a period of years. The development was not as successful as the Lant and Smith estates nearer the city, discussed on page 86. Some plots were bought up and developed in larger blocks during the 1850s like those top-shops seen above on the right, at the corner of Cromwell Street and Red Lane. Unfortunately, these particularly well-built top-shops did not survive the heavy bombing of the area during the Second World War. The houses on the left were only built at the end of the nineteenth century. Similarly, the other houses in the estate also suffered in the War and in the post-war period and few of the houses in Cromwell Street are still standing. The view below gives a flavour of its original appearance. It is taken by the junction with Bright Street. To begin with it was very underdeveloped with only a few houses on the right and one on the left, having been built in the mid-nineteenth century but they did include some top-shops. Almost all the houses down the left (east) side were built at the end of the nineteenth century.

Cromwell Street 1907 (E.R.)

25, Cobden Street 1912 (Stoke Portrait Co)   **42, Henrietta Street c1910 (Anon.)**

Here are two contrasting views of terraced houses from the Stoney Stanton area showing the main differences between the sort of working-class housing erected in the mid-nineteenth century compared to those at the end of the Victorian era and the Edwardian period. Some of the changes are due to fashion, but others have been forced upon developers by the introduction of building regulations aimed at improving living conditions. There are clear similarities in the frontages of the houses, both having two sash windows with four lights and a front door off-set and the panelling of the door itself, down to the number plate, is almost the same. But 25 Cobden Street dates from the 1850s when the classical style that had been popular with the landed gentry for more than 150 years had been re-interpreted for the most humble terraced houses. The design of the wooden surround to the door has echoes of the stone pilasters, capitals and cornices found at the entrance of the finest country houses. The decorative keystone lintels above the windows follow a similar theme. The windows lights in both houses are much larger than earlier in the century thanks to improvements in glass technology allowing it to be cheaper and less weighty so the glazing bars could become thinner. They also both follow the classical proportions of the Georgian era. Superficially it would seem that by 1903 when 42, Henrietta Street was built that standards had decreased; the lack of detailing on the door surround and the unelaborated stone lintels over the windows seem to be a backward step, although the transom, the window above the door, has been retained.

But some improvements are obvious, such as the small front garden as a result of the building line being set back from the pavement, the small front wall with decorative ironwork. When Coventry terraces from the mid-nineteenth century were set back from the pavement they tended to have just iron railings rather than a half brick wall. The Henrietta Street front door also has two steps back from the pavement giving better protection from the weather. This was partly a function of the requirement for the floorboards to be no longer set on the ground but to have a six-inch ventilation space underneath. Both buildings use the Flemish bond style of brickwork, which is where bricks alternate between being laid at right angles to each other which indicates that walls are built of two layers of brick but without a cavity wall. Improvements in standards were gradually forced upon builders by a series of Acts from local and central government during the Victorian era. Some were less obvious than others. They laid down minimum sizes for rooms as well as sanitation, banning back-to-back housing and shared toilets. A minor point to note is the typical use of brick sets for the pavement in Cobden Street in the mid-nineteenth century that were being replaced by large paving stones by the start of the twentieth century (see Station Street West page 40). The woman shown at Cobden Street is Margaret Angliss aged 56 who had a hard life as a widow for 12 years. She had eight children, the first two out of wedlock, three later died. None of the houses on this west side of Cobden Street is still standing.

8. Upper Stoney Stanton Road and Courthouse Green

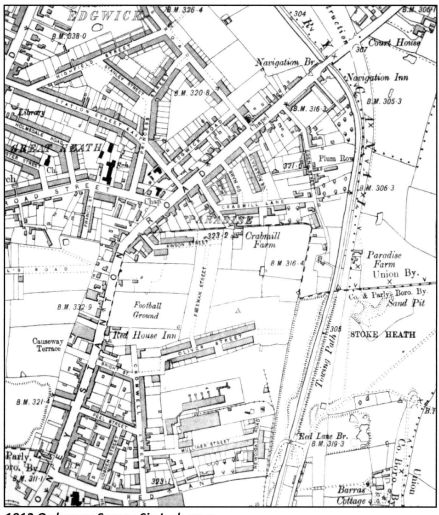

1912 Ordnance Survey Six Inch map

Stoney Stanton Road enters the parish of Foleshill at its junction with Red Lane. The boundary then follows the eastern side of the road before branching off towards Stoke Heath by the junction with Awson Street. This section of the book deals with the northern stretch from where the old Red Lane pub was situated up to the canal by the site of the Navigation Inn. Here Stoney Stanton Road becomes Bell Green Road through Courthouse Green and onto Bell Green itself.

Although this northern part of the road follows an older course than the southern section, its straight lines reflect the 1831 turnpike upgrade from mere tracks across the heath. When the canal was built a useful route passing this area was blocked in a couple of places. It ran south from Spring Road in Little Heath across the Stoney Stanton Road, into Eden Street and onto Swan Lane. Near where it would have joined Swan Lane was Paradise Farm. This part of Stoney Stanton Road is known as Paradise, but whether the farm gave its name to the district or vice versa, the meaning of the word as used here is a mystery. The biblical origin is assumed by those who named Eden Street (originally Paradise Row) and its pub, the Adam and Eve. Its use as a place name is not uncommon, especially in agriculture as a field name. This normally is a reflection of the fertility of the land, though sometimes used ironically. This may be why Paradise Farm was so named.

The canal brought belated benefits to this part of Stoney Stanton Road with early nineteenth century developments around the intersection of the road and the canal. Goods could be conveniently transferred from the canal to the road and vice versa, so a wharf was built, which in turn attracted various businesses. By 1824 Paradise Row (later Eden St), was laid out, with building plots advertised in local papers. At about the same time the Navigation Inn opened for business. By the mid-nineteenth century, weaver's top-shops had been built both on and off this stretch of upper Stoney Stanton Road. Unfortunately, the area was badly affected by wartime bombing and subsequent redevelopment, so much so that there are hardly any buildings dating back to the nineteenth century. Even the Navigation Inn has gone, so the Adam and Eve pub in Eden Street is to be cherished as one of those rare surviving buildings from the first half of the nineteenth century, especially as it contains adjoining old cottages that it took over in the 1930s.

Red House Inn, 483 Stoney Stanton Road c1913 (Anon.)

The Red House Inn has a long history stretching back at least to the eighteenth century, though that was not the building shown here which dates from 1858. The significance of this enlarged building seems to have given rise to an unofficial renaming of the length of the road through Paradise as 'Red House Road' as it appears for the first time in the newspapers of that year. However, by 1889 newspaper reports commented that the use of this address, when it was officially Stoney Stanton Road, meant that it was proving difficult for some locals to register for a vote! The pub was associated with the Venn family for much of the second half of the nineteenth century and up to the Second World War. As a result of war

damage another rebuild was carried out in the 1950s, set back behind the building shown here. But after a later incarnation as 'Fatty Arbuckles' nightclub it closed in 1995 and is now the site of Rathbone Court, a housing development.

This is a family snapshot from the Aston family of their house in the 1930s, opposite Bryn Road. 40-year-old Lucy Aston is standing outside the building. It is a comparatively well-preserved example of a mid-nineteenth century house that has some interesting similarities and differences to that of 25 Cobden Street discussed on page 92. Though it has all the characteristics of a terraced house it has been constructed as a separate building. It abuts an earlier and simpler cottage on its left, more typical of the cottages found all over the Foleshill area from the late eighteenth century. This mixture of building types fronting Foleshill's roads and lanes contrasts with the more formally organised developments found mainly from the late-nineteenth century onwards. The style of the front door and its surround, as well as the windows and their keystone lintels, are almost identical to 25 Cobden Street. However, the delicate fluting in the door surrounds and the more pronounced panels in the lintels suggest a slightly higher status. The setback building line and, for the time, the atypical garden wall and ironwork reinforce this point. Like so many other buildings in this part of Stoney Stanton Road, it did not survive the War, making it difficult to appreciate its nineteenth century origins except though surviving photographs.

566 Stoney Stanton Road c1935 (Aston)

Stoney Stanton Road c1955 (Anon.)

On the corner of Awson Street and 583 and 585 Stoney Stanton Road is Stevenson's chemist business. It survived the war broadly unscathed, but the two shops to the south (577 and 579) were badly damaged and in 1951 were described as being in ruins. They were repaired by the time of this photograph but the other houses in the terrace were too badly damaged and just a gap remains. Lily Stevenson, the daughter of the Chemist caused controversy pre-war when in 1937 she applied to become the first female freeman of the city on finishing her apprenticeship as a chemist. Her legal battle went on until 1944 when the principle of female freemen was finally accepted.

Herbert D Parham Butchers Delivery Wagon at Barnacle c1912 (Anon.)

Just beyond in the junction with Station Street East, at 528 Stoney Stanton Road was Parham's butcher shop; the family also had a branch at 404 Foleshill Road. They were still trading in 1940 but were next door to one another in Foleshill Road. Herbert Dunn Parham had his base at the village of Barnacle, five miles away. In 1911 he was living with his widowed mother in 1911 in Holmesdale Road, Foleshill and at the tender age of 24 had two employees. This could well be him in the bowler hat with his delivery men on the wagon which has 'Herbert D Parham English Meat Purveyor Barnacle' painted on the side. It appears that he might have soon bought a motor van as he was prosecuted for driving such a vehicle in a careless way in Bedworth in July 1915. By 1940 although was still alongside the family in Foleshill he also had another shop at 74 Coventry Road, Exhall.

A City bound Tram on Stoney Stanton Road 1937 (Priestley)

The contrast between these two views demonstrates the damage both physical and social to the community of Paradise by war and redevelopment. The 1930s view shows the tram service still operating and the terraces of shops and houses are only interrupted by the junctions of side roads. The tram is heading into town just past the Station Street East junction on the left with the Crabmill Lane junction further back on the right. A variety of shops such as Frost's boot shop on the right offered a range of services to the area. The fact that this was an active and well-served community is very clear.

Twenty years later and the damage caused by the Second World War is apparent in the view below. Almost all the houses on the left from the Station Street East junction have gone as well as a section beyond Crabmill Lane on the right. Some improvements have been attempted such as the creation of mini-parks where gaps had been made by wartime destruction. Also, the Royal Oak, partially shown on the extreme right of both photographs, was rebuilt further back from the road but it was closed in 2010 and is now a food store. It appears if so many of the subsequent developments on the buildings flanking the road seem to have been haphazard and lack the pre-war coherence.

631 Stoney Stanton Road c1955 (Anon.)

Paradise Post Office, Stoney Stanton Road 1912 (Anon.)

The collection of buildings above is at the junction of Cross Road. The shop in the centre is Paradise Post Office at 590 Stoney Stanton Road and three doors down, on the corner of Cross Road is 596 Stoney Stanton Road where Daniel Wagstaff runs his small general store, built as an extension to the house into the front garden. All the houses date from the mid-nineteenth century or earlier, the cottages being the oldest with each of their three section casement opening windows being made of 24 separate pieces of glass, necessary before technology reduced the price of larger pieces. Behind the cottages, in Cross Road, can be seen part of Paradise Primitive Methodist Chapel built in 1865, replacing an earlier one built in 1828. Beyond this junction with Cross Road were nine weavers' top-shops, three still occupied by weavers in 1912.

The equally impressive Sunday school associated with the chapel was built along its western side. It was opened in 1907 at a cost of £1,900 and the postcard was produced in celebration of the event. In the Second World War, the Sunday school building was taken over by the Home and the front of the chapel suffered bomb damage. Broad Street Chapel which had been destroyed in the War joined with the Paradise Chapel and it became the Edgwick Methodist Chapel. It has since been demolished and from 1978 the Sunday School building has been used as the Shree Mandhata Samaj Community Hall.

Paradise Primitive Methodist School, Stoney Stanton Road 1907 (JE Slapoffski)

Weavers Arms, Courthouse Green c1907 (J.P.)

Given the number of weavers in Foleshill, it is surprising this is the only pub mentioning the industry in the area. It seems appropriate that it has expanded from a single cottage to incorporate one of the neighbouring three-storey weaver's cottages. The pub was located where the present pub is to be found today, on the north side of the road beyond Proffitt Avenue on the way to Bell Green. The old pub was demolished in the 1930s when the current pub was erected to its rear. None of the buildings shown survives today (many in the foreground were demolished when the pub was extended) only the line of the road is the same. The few old Courthouse Green buildings that can still be seen now are along the south side of the road.

Nearer Bell Green some of the post-war changes are apparent in the mid-1950s postcard below. Old buildings have been demolished and together with the surrounding green fields, provided the land for extending Coventry City Council's 1930s Courthouse Green Estate. The new buildings can be seen in the background; in the foreground is Armfield Street to the immediate left and a few of the old Courthouse Green cottages still surviving on the right. Today only the two cottages on the far right remain, much altered. The taller one displays the top shop window of the local ribbon weaving industry but the impracticality of such a large window losing so much heat has triumphed over heritage so the roofline has been lowered in the course of modernisation. It is an appropriate way to finish this book with a scene that sums up so many of the characteristic changes to Foleshill over the last two centuries.

Bell Green Road, Courthouse Green c1955 (Landscape)

Readers Aids: Doing Your Own Research

Secondary Sources

Some interesting miscellaneous historical facts and episodes from Foleshill's history can be found in Gordon Cowley's *Folks Hill: A History of Foleshill Warwickshire 1745 – 1945* (2000) and David McGrory's *The Illustrated History of Coventry's Suburbs* (2003). *A History of Warwickshire, Volume 8* (1969) in The Victoria History of the Counties of England series is the best for a detailed history of Foleshill (pp. 57 – 70), but is not such an easy read.

Primary Sources

Some of the best material is still waiting to be uncovered in the Coventry History Centre at The Herbert Art Gallery and Museum. With a bit of patience you can find the original plans for your house and your street and, with luck, maybe the deeds. These can reveal who built it and a little about the people who lived there. The best starting point is the excellent database of records. This is available online at www.coventrycollections.org . Even better is to use the standalone version at the History Centre that allows searches within searches and organisation of results by date or type of record. This should help you find the plans to your house, but unfortunately some plans were destroyed in the war, especially amongst the earliest ones from the 1890s. Also the database does not currently list plans beyond the mid-1930s. However, the complete list is also available on microfiche, organised by street, and is quite up to date. This is also the starting point for a house deed search. The History Centre's full set of Street Directories can also show who lived in the property as more houses were rented than owner occupied in the first half of the last century.

For the broader picture about activities of the City Corporation (Its official name until 1974 when it became the City Council) there are some excellent minute books. The 'Minutes of the General Works Committee' date from the second half of the nineteenth into the twentieth century, providing insights into the development of the all the City's suburbs. Note, however, that Foleshill was only gradually included in these as the City boundary extended. Nevertheless there are Foleshill Parish Council records and later Foleshill District Council records available.

The Land Tax Assessment was a short lived government initiative just before the First World War that bears comparison with the Doomsday Book in its scope of detailing all property holding in the country and its worth. The Values Books include of details of owners and occupiers organised by street and are lodged in the History Centre. For fuller details it is necessary to visit the National Archives in London.

Access to old maps is easy in the History Centre for the original paper versions. The internet offers a few useful sources for older maps such as www.old-maps.co.uk which allows you to examine a location over the years using the various scales of Ordnance Survey maps. Also, the Scottish National Library site (maps.nls.uk) has the facility to compare old maps with the modern equivalent aerial view. Those used in the introductions to each section of this book are taken mainly from the Ordnance Survey 1912 Six Inch Series.

The index focuses upon people and places. Where there is an appropriate illustration, for instance a photograph, drawing, plan or map then the page number will appear in **bold**.

Places